Series editor: Philip Prowse

Emergency Murder

Janet McGiffin

CAMBRIDGE
UNIVERSITY PRESS

CAMBRIDGE UNIVERSITY PRESS
Cambridge, New York, Melbourne, Madrid, Cape Town, Singapore, São Paulo, Delhi

Cambridge University Press
The Edinburgh Building, Cambridge CB2 8RU, UK

www.cambridge.org
Information on this title: www.cambridge.org/9780521536622

First published 2003
10th printing 2009

Printed in Italy by L.E.G.O. S.p.A.

A catalogue record for this publication is available from the British Library

ISBN 978-0-521-53662-2 paperback
ISBN 978-0-521-68644-0 paperback plus audio CD pack

Contents

Chapter 1	Death in the Emergency Room	6
Chapter 2	Doubts	10
Chapter 3	Poison	13
Chapter 4	An unexpected visit	19
Chapter 5	Suspicions	23
Chapter 6	Grabowski gets no answers	29
Chapter 7	Hank gets angry	34
Chapter 8	Maxine and Grabowski talk	40
Chapter 9	Attack at the tennis club	45
Chapter 10	A new suspect	50
Chapter 11	Lies	55
Chapter 12	Another attack	60
Chapter 13	Lavelle knows more	63
Chapter 14	Maxine investigates	69
Chapter 15	24th Street and North Avenue	76
Chapter 16	Hank takes action	81
Chapter 17	Maxine finds the truth	87
Chapter 18	Post mortem	92

Characters

Dr. Maxine Cassidy: a doctor at Mercy Hospital ER
Shirley: a nurse at Mercy Hospital
Detective Grabowski
Hank Myer: a surgeon
Nanette Myer: Hank's wife
Aaron: Maxine's colleague
Stanley: Maxine's colleague
Lavelle: a patient
Dr. Virginia Gaust: a researcher at Marquette University
Charlie: Virginia's research assistant

Virginia's
house

Hank's house

Maxine's
house

North 20th Street

North 25th Street

Public
Health
Clinic

Mercy
hospital

North Avenue

M I L W A U K E E

Lake
Michigan

Marquette University

N

C A N A D A

Lake
Superior

Lake
Huron

WISCONSIN

Lake Michigan

Detroit

Milwaukee

Chicago

U.S.A.

Grabowski's
house

Chapter 1 *Death in the Emergency Room*

It was midnight on a hot July Sunday in Milwaukee, Wisconsin. Dr. Maxine Cassidy was still at work at Mercy Hospital Emergency Room. Most of the people she took care of in the ER lived nearby in the rough area of Milwaukee. After eight hours on her feet, Maxine was exhausted. Shirley, the emergency room nurse, handed her a cup of coffee.

"Are you sorry you left your research job at Marquette University?" asked Shirley. "You've only worked here six months and already you look beat."

Shirley sat down at the reception desk and watched the ER doors for new patients. Shirley was a big woman who could handle any kind of trouble. Maxine was small and slim with short brown curly hair.

"Coffee break is over, Doctor," said Shirley, nodding toward the woman who was coming through the doors. "Lavelle's here again."

Lavelle was a young woman who lived near Mercy Hospital. She often came into the ER. This evening, she had a deep cut on her arm where she had fallen on the sidewalk. Maxine sewed it up and put on a bandage.

"Come back in a few days, Lavelle, and I'll check it," Maxine said.

Suddenly, Shirley saw that a woman had just entered the ER. She looked very sick and as if she was about to fall. Shirley ran toward the woman. "Quick! Help!" she shouted to Maxine as the woman fell into her arms. Maxine ran to help and together they carried the woman toward the examination table.

The woman was wearing a red wig, a black leather miniskirt, and a thin pink sweater, and was holding a large black shoulder bag.

As Maxine and Shirley helped the woman onto the examination table, her red wig fell off. She had short black hair that was wet with sweat. The woman lifted her head. "Maxine," she whispered. "Where's Maxine?"

Maxine gasped. "It's Nanette Myer – Dr. Hank Myer's wife!"

Dr. Hank Myer was a busy surgeon with many patients. He did surgery in five different hospitals, including Mercy Hospital. He was also on the Board of Marquette University, and sat on the Research Review Committee at Marquette University. His clinic was in the richest part of Milwaukee, near his home. He and his wife, Nanette, lived in an huge white brick house next to Lake Michigan.

"Nanette Myer?" asked Shirley. "Are you sure? Why is she wearing those clothes?" Shirley and Maxine helped the woman sit on the examination table.

"Help me! I feel sick," she said. She couldn't sit up by herself. She kept falling against Shirley.

"It *is* Nanette," Maxine answered Shirley. "But why did she come to Mercy Hospital ER? There are hospitals nearer her home."

"I can't breathe!" Nanette whispered.

Maxine was looking at Nanette's arms and legs, but couldn't find any obvious injury. "I don't know what's wrong with her!"

"When did you get sick?" Shirley asked Nanette.

"About ten minutes ago. A taxi stopped for me, thank God," she answered.

"Have you ever felt like this before?" asked Maxine.

"Never."

"Are you taking any medicine?"

"Yes. It's in my shoulder bag." Nanette reached for the large black bag but it fell on the floor. Shirley picked it up. She pulled out a long red dress. She also pulled out lipstick, blue eye shadow, and two bottles of pills. Shirley read from the side of the bottles: "Carisoprodol, Ferrous Sulphate."

Nanette leaned all her weight on Maxine, with her head on Maxine's shoulder. Maxine shook Nanette's arm. "Where were you tonight? What did you eat?"

"I didn't eat anything. I took a pill," Nanette said.

"Which pill? A pill from your purse?" Shirley asked.

Suddenly Nanette cried out, "I can't breathe! Everything's gone dark!"

Maxine and Shirley helped her lie down. Maxine looked into Nanette's eyes. The black centers of the eyes were equal in size but they were moving in different directions. Maxine felt the side of Nanette's hand.

"Her nerves and muscles are weak," Maxine said to Shirley. Suddenly Maxine realized that Nanette had stopped breathing.

"Get the emergency medical team here!" Maxine shouted to the ER receptionist.

In less than a minute the emergency medical team ran through the door – a heart specialist, a technician to work the medical equipment, and a nurse.

For the next fifteen minutes, the medical team tried to

make Nanette's heart beat and make Nanette breathe again. Finally the heart specialist held up his hand.

"She's gone. Turn off the machines," the specialist ordered.

"She's dead," whispered Shirley. She wrote down the time of death and signed her name. Then she got a blue sheet and covered Nanette.

Chapter 2 *Doubts*

Maxine was at home in bed, asleep, when the ringing phone woke her. She stared at the clock: 3:16 AM.

"Yes? Hello?" Maxine said into the phone.

"Maxine, thank God. It's Hank." He sounded upset and a little drunk. "What happened to Nanette? My receptionist called me. What the hell happened?"

Maxine turned on the lamp and sat up. "Hank, I tried to reach you, but your cell phone was turned off. I'm so sorry to tell you. Nanette came into Mercy Hospital ER about midnight. She was very sick. We did everything we could."

"What? I don't understand."

"Nanette said she felt sick," began Maxine. "She couldn't breathe. Her muscles were weak. While I was examining her, her heart stopped. The heart specialist tried everything he could, but . . . Hank, I'm so sorry."

"Why did Nanette go to Mercy Hospital? There are hospitals nearer to our home!"

"We could ask the taxi driver," suggested Maxine.

"Taxi? What happened to her car?" Hank's voice shook.

"I don't know."

"Nanette was healthy," Hank said. "She never had any serious illnesses. There was nothing wrong with her heart."

"Shall I order an autopsy?" Maxine asked.

Hank didn't answer right away. An autopsy meant Nanette's body would be kept for tests. An autopsy was a good idea when a person died with no obvious cause. As a doctor, Hank knew this. But it was a hard decision. And it might delay the burial.

"All right," Hank said finally. "Who'll do the autopsy?"

"Aaron. Here at Mercy Hospital pathology lab. I'll ask him to do it as quickly as he can."

Maxine hung up the phone and turned off the lamp. She could still hear Hank's voice in her ears. The man had a physical effect on her – and on everyone else. He had a power which either drew people or frightened them away. She had known Hank for five years. He'd been very kind to her during her divorce six months ago. Hank had suggested that Maxine take a leave of absence from her job at Marquette University. He suggested that she go to work at Mercy Hospital ER. Hank was right. At Mercy Hospital, Maxine was able to put the divorce behind her.

As she went back to sleep, Maxine thought about the last time she had seen Nanette. It had been the weekend before, at Hank and Nanette's lovely home by Lake Michigan. It had been a barbecue party by the swimming pool. Most of the guests were doctors that Maxine knew. Some were professors from Marquette University. Maxine thought about Nanette, moving amongst her guests, laughing and talking. It was difficult to think that Nanette was now dead.

Monday was Maxine's day off, but she called Aaron at the hospital and asked him to do an autopsy on Nanette. Aaron promised he would do it by the next day.

Late Tuesday afternoon, Maxine was back at ER when Aaron phoned from the Mercy Hospital pathology lab with the results of the autopsy.

"The autopsy didn't show anything unusual. Nanette died of heart failure," he said.

"And the pills we found in her shoulder bag? Did you do tests on them?" Maxine asked.

"Yes. We found nothing unusual. They were just what they said."

"Thanks for telling me, Aaron."

He didn't hang up the phone. "Did you know Nanette well?" he asked. "I saw you at Hank and Nanette's party last week."

"I know Hank better. He was on the Research Review Committee at Marquette. He reviewed my research each year. He and Nanette invited me to a lot of parties at their house."

An hour later, the ER was empty again. Maxine signed all the reports. She sat down in the armchair to drink coffee. Shirley sat next to her, keeping an eye on the entrance to the ER.

"I heard that the autopsy results showed that Nanette died of heart failure," Shirley said. "Do you believe that such a young woman could die of heart failure?"

"Well, it's possible, but . . ." Maxine began, but the phone rang before she could finish. She answered it.

Maxine listened for a minute and then hung up. "That was Hank's receptionist. Hank wants me to come to Nanette's burial tomorrow," she told Shirley.

Shirley raised an eyebrow. "You know Hank well?" she asked.

"We're just friends," Maxine said sharply.

Chapter 3 *Poison*

Nanette was buried on Wednesday in a grassy space shaded by tall trees. Birds sang and a light wind from Lake Michigan cooled the July heat. Most people at the burial were doctors and their wives, dressed in expensive suits. They seemed more curious than sad, or just doing their professional duty. There were also many professors from Marquette University, including Maxine's colleague, Dr. Virginia Gaust.

The reception after the burial was at Hank's house. People filled the beautiful house, talking and eating. Maxine carried her plate into the library where there was a grand piano and tall bookcases. The walls were covered in the same Chinese material as the comfortable sofas and armchairs. French doors led outside to the garden and the swimming pool. Maxine sat down at the shining library table. Then she felt a hand on her shoulder.

"Virginia!" Maxine exclaimed. She liked Virginia because she was friendly and full of energy. They had been colleagues for years and had shared the same lab at Marquette. Virginia did brilliant research for new drugs.

Virginia set her plate of sandwiches on the library table and sat down. "Maxine, I've been leaving messages for you at Mercy Hospital. Why don't you call me back?"

Maxine took a bite of her sandwich. "I'm sorry. I've been working so hard lately."

"What do you do besides work at the ER? Have you met

any nice men? Are you dating anyone?" Virginia leaned forward.

"No, Virginia. I'm still learning how to be an ER doctor. After three years doing research at Marquette, I'd forgotten what a heartbeat sounded like," replied Maxine.

Virginia raised an eyebrow. "I still don't understand why you left Marquette. You were doing excellent research."

"It's only a temporary job at Mercy Hospital. I need something different to help me start my new life as a single woman. My research is waiting for me and in six months, I'll come back."

Virginia started searching for more news. "I heard you were the doctor in the ER when Nanette died. Was she really wearing a tight leather skirt and a red wig?"

Maxine looked around nervously. "Where did you hear that?"

"There are no secrets in hospitals, dear. There are always people watching. I heard that Nanette died of heart failure."

Maxine frowned. "That's what the report of the autopsy said. But I think it's a mistake."

"Why?" asked Virginia.

"Because Nanette was a healthy woman. Hank said she had never been seriously ill. There was no reason for her to die suddenly of heart failure."

Virginia nodded. "True. She used to play tennis with me at the tennis club. She was always giving parties. Do you know why she suddenly got so sick?"

"I tried to ask her where she had been before she came to the ER," Maxine went on. "But I didn't have time to talk to her before she died."

"Didn't Nanette tell you anything at all?" asked Virginia.

Maxine tried to remember. "Nanette said something about a pill. But Aaron tested all the pills in her purse. He said there was nothing unusual."

"Do you know why she was wearing those strange clothes?" Virginia asked.

"No." Maxine leaned forward and asked softly, "Have you heard anything strange about Nanette?"

"Not a word," replied Virginia, loudly. "But I saw you giving Hank hungry looks at the burial. Are you having an affair with him?"

Maxine gasped. "Absolutely not! And don't start telling people anything about Hank and me. We're just good friends." Maxine stood up quickly and went towards the front door. Hank was shaking hands with people who were leaving. Hank's face was pale and his eyes were red. He held both Maxine's hands. She kissed his cheek.

"I'll call you," she promised, and hurried out into the hot sun.

Ahead of her was an old friend, Stanley, a brilliant professor and researcher in biochemistry at Marquette. Maxine had talked to him a lot about her own research when she needed advice. "I need to talk," said Maxine.

"You're worried about Nanette's death," Stanley guessed.

They walked a short distance to a café and ordered some coffee.

"There's something wrong, but I don't know what," Maxine began. "I don't even know how to start looking for the answer. In the ER, I thought that Nanette had heart failure. The heart specialist agreed. The autopsy said that she died of natural causes. But now I have started to think that her heart failure was caused by something that was not natural. I think we don't know the whole story."

Stanley listened patiently as Maxine explained the details.

"I feel like a failure," Maxine admitted. "Nanette came to Mercy Hospital ER and called my name. She thought I could save her. But I couldn't. Maybe I even did something wrong. Maybe it's my fault that she died."

"I'm a researcher, not an ER doctor," said Stanley, "but I work in biochemistry so I can make an educated guess. Nanette got sick very quickly and her body shut down very fast. Her nervous system shut down first, which caused her muscles to get weak. To me, that sounds like poison."

"Poison!" exclaimed Maxine. "Impossible! Aaron didn't find any poison when he did the autopsy."

"You can't find many poisons unless you do specific tests for them. Try to find a poison that affects the nerves and then causes heart failure. Like a snake poison, for example."

"I don't understand," Maxine said. "How could she get hold of poison?"

"Before you worry about that, you have to find out which poison killed her," Stanley advised.

"How?" Maxine asked. "She's buried."

"Ask Aaron if he saved any blood from the autopsy."

"I'll do that," said Maxine. She stood up to leave.

"Wait," said Stanley. "Is this the right thing to do? Is it important to find out how Nanette died? The autopsy report says heart failure. Hank seems satisfied with that. Maybe Nanette should be left in peace."

Maxine drove to Mercy Hospital ER and arrived with enough time to go to the pathology lab and talk to Aaron.

Aaron was doing an autopsy when Maxine pushed open the swinging doors of the pathology lab. He was wearing gloves, a green mask over his fat cheeks, and a large green surgical gown over his clothes. Maxine stood by the door and held a mask over her mouth.

"I want to talk to you about Nanette's autopsy results," said Maxine.

"Her report's in the top drawer over there," Aaron answered.

"I don't want the report. I want you to do another test. I think Nanette was poisoned."

Aaron stopped cutting. "Poisoned!" he exclaimed. "With what?"

"A nerve poison."

Aaron laughed. "Like snake poison?"

"Maybe. Can you test for a poison that weakens the nerves and muscles, like what happened to Nanette? I want to find out why Nanette died suddenly of heart failure and testing for nerve poison is one way to start looking," Maxine explained.

Aaron raised his thick eyebrows. "Everyone is satisfied with the autopsy results. Including Hank."

"I'm not," Maxine said. "A thirty-five-year-old woman should not suddenly die of heart failure."

"Are you worried that you did the right thing in the ER? Be careful, Maxine. If I do another test, you might find out things you don't want to know."

"Like what?"

"Like you made a mistake in the ER." Aaron began

17

cutting at the body on the table again. "You know Hank well, don't you?" he commented.

"I know him casually," Maxine said. She changed the subject. "What do we do now?"

"I saved some blood when I did the autopsy. The bottle is in the freezer."

"Do you always save blood from autopsies?" Maxine asked.

"Yes, for a few months anyway. Sometimes the police have come in here months after someone died and have told me to do another test."

"How long will it take to get an answer?" Maxine asked.

"About a week. I'll have to send the blood to a special lab in Texas."

"Thanks Aaron. I owe you."

"You certainly do, Maxine."

Maxine was still thinking about her conversation with Aaron while she drove home after work. She stopped the car in her driveway and turned off the car engine and lights. Then she stopped for a moment, her hand on the key. A man was waiting in the shadows by her front door.

"Hank." She got out of her car and hurried to meet him in the warm night. Maxine put her arms around him.

"Maxine," he said quietly. "My house is too empty. I can't go home. Let me stay here. I need a friend."

She hugged him. "Stay as long as you want," she said. She made a bed for him on the couch, but they sat talking long into the night.

Chapter 4 *An unexpected visit*

"Maxine!" called Shirley. "Aaron wants you to come to the pathology lab. Fast!"

Maxine ran down the stairs to Mercy Hospital pathology lab. It had been only four days since Aaron had sent the blood from Nanette's autopsy to Texas. Did he have an answer already?

When Maxine pushed open the swinging doors, Aaron was sitting at his desk. Across from him was a man with his back to the door. Aaron's face looked pale.

"Someone called the police," he announced.

The man turned, and looked surprised to see her.

Maxine smiled. "Detective Grabowski!"

Maxine was pleased to see Grabowski. She had met him a couple of months ago when he had come to the ER, injured. He had asked her out for coffee afterward and they had gotten along well. But she hadn't seen him since then. He worked long hours and he didn't seem to have time for a social life. She was glad to see him again now. He was handsome, with dark hair, an untidy moustache, and muscles that showed through his shirt.

"What's the problem?" Maxine pulled up a chair and sat down.

Aaron answered. "The lab in Texas sent Nanette's report to the police."

Grabowski interrupted. "Somebody at the lab decided that the Milwaukee police should know that a poison called tetrodotoxin was in a blood test sent from Mercy Hospital."

"What!" Maxine gasped. "Tetrodotoxin?"

"Your idea about a nerve poison was right, Maxine," Aaron said. "There was enough poison in that blood to kill six people. But it's amazing that it was tetrodotoxin."

"Tetrodotoxin?" Maxine repeated. Her voice shook.

Grabowski frowned. "This was your idea, to do the test for nerve poison? Why is it so amazing that it was tetrodotoxin? I've never heard of it."

Maxine nodded. "Neither have most people. I know about it because I used it in my research at Marquette University only six months ago."

Grabowski frowned. "Let's start again. How long did you use the poison in your research?"

"I started my research three years ago and finished six months ago."

"Did anyone else use this poison?" Grabowski asked.

"I prefer to think of it as a research drug, if that's alright," said Maxine.

"OK. Just tell me who else used it."

"My research assistant, Charlie. He used it when he was helping me with my research. Do you want to know about my research?"

Grabowski held up a hand. "Not yet. How did you and the other researchers get the drug?"

"I got mine from a chemical company in Chicago. They sell research drugs to laboratories. But the chemical comes from a fish called the puffer fish which are used in medical research a lot. They're also rare and beautiful fish and some people buy them for their fish tanks at home."

Grabowski was writing in his notebook. "Who knew you had this poison?"

"My research wasn't secret," Maxine said. "Lots of my students came to my lab to watch my experiments. Also, I wrote reports on my research that the university keeps. The drug company may keep my reports secret, but Marquette University puts that information in a file. I suppose anyone could get hold of those reports. I gave talks about my research, too."

Maxine's pager beeped. "I'm needed in the ER," she said and hurried out the door. On her way to the ER, Maxine thought over the situation. Nanette had been poisoned by tetrodotoxin. Could it have been an accident? Had the poison come from Maxine's laboratory? But how?

When she got to the ER, Maxine phoned Charlie. Charlie was a Ph.D. student who worked as a research assistant as well as studying. He worked day and night and often slept in the lab.

Maxine let the phone ring ten times. Finally someone picked it up.

"Charlie?" Maxine said. "Is that you?"

"Umm."

"Charlie, this is Maxine. I have to see you. Can I come to your lab tonight when I get off work, after midnight?"

"Sure. I'll still be here." He hung up.

Shirley was listening. "Is this call connected with Nanette's murder?"

"Who says it's murder?" Maxine demanded.

"Got to be murder when that good-looking Detective Grabowski gets involved. You're friendly with Hank, aren't you? Did that make the detective suspicious about you?"

"Certainly not!" said Maxine. "I know Hank because we're both doctors. Hank is on the Research Review Committee at Marquette and he does surgery here. I've worked with him in both places."

"And you go to parties at his house," said Shirley.

"So do a lot of people."

"Not me," said Shirley.

Chapter 5 *Suspicions*

At midnight, Maxine left the hospital and walked to her car. The air was hot and humid. It would be cooler at her house near Lake Michigan where there was always a light wind off the lake. Maxine was tired and wanted to go home to bed but she had to talk to Charlie.

The buildings of Marquette University were dark among the trees. Maxine parked her car on the street and walked through the trees to the biochemistry building where Charlie was working. She opened the door with her key. She had not returned her key when she left six months before. She thought she would be coming back.

A thin line of light was under Charlie's lab door. Maxine opened the door. Then she stopped, surprised. Grabowski was leaning against the computer.

"What are you doing here, Grabowski?" Maxine demanded.

"I phoned Charlie this afternoon, after you called him," replied Grabowski. "He told me you were coming here tonight. I decided to come, too. I wanted to find out why you're in a hurry to talk to him," replied Grabowski.

Charlie looked nervous. "Detective Grabowski was asking about your research, Maxine. What's this all about?"

"I found out today that Nanette was poisoned. With tetrodotoxin," Maxine said.

Charlie's face turned pale. "Poisoned? How?"

"That's what we're trying to find out," said Grabowski as he opened his notebook. "No-one in any Milwaukee university is doing research that uses puffer fish or tetrodotoxin. That means this lab is the only place we know that definitely had the poison. That puts you in a very bad position, Maxine. How did you get your tetrodotoxin?"

Charlie answered. "We mailed a chemical supply company a document that proved we were a university laboratory. Then the company sent us the tetrodotoxin by special mail."

"Where did you keep the poison when it got here?"

Maxine answered. "I locked it in my desk."

Grabowski turned to Charlie. "Did you have a key to that desk?"

Charlie looked nervous. "Yes. But I didn't need it. Maxine usually didn't lock it. She forgets to lock anything. Probably her car is not locked right now."

Maxine's face turned red. The night she had gone out for coffee with Grabowski after work, she had returned to her car and found it unlocked. Grabowski had advised her to be more careful in the future.

"Tell me more about tetrodotoxin," Grabowski said. "How did you use it in your experiments?"

Maxine explained. "My research was about heart medicine. I used tetrodotoxin in the research. It stops the heart beat without killing the heart so that experiments can be done on the heart. We took a rat's heart and we . . ."

"I don't want the details," interrupted Grabowski. "Does tetrodotoxin have a smell or a taste?"

"It came as a clear liquid in small glass tubes," answered

Maxine. "It didn't smell. As far as taste, I never want to find out."

"What did you do with it in your experiments?"

"I opened one tube and mixed some with water," Maxine said. "I used this solution in my experiments. At the end of each day I poured it down the sink."

"Did you ever have any poison left in the tube at the end of the day?" Grabowski asked.

"Sometimes," Maxine said.

"Where did you put it?" Grabowski asked.

"In the lab refrigerator."

"Who used the lab refrigerator?" Grabowski exclaimed.

"Every researcher kept chemicals in the lab refrigerator," Maxine answered.

"That's right." Charlie came to her support. "The head of our department has asked the university to buy us another lab refrigerator, but so far they haven't."

"Who is the head of your department?" Grabowski asked.

Charlie replied. "Dr. Virginia Gaust. Her office is down the hall. She uses this lab for her research too. When Maxine worked here, all three of us shared it."

"Show me this refrigerator," Grabowski ordered.

Charlie led the way down the dark hall and pushed open a door on the right. Maxine unlocked the refrigerator.

"Who has a key for this refrigerator?" Grabowski asked.

"Well, all the professors who are doing any research and all research assistants," Maxine answered.

"So any one of them could steal anything from here?" Grabowski said.

"No-one has ever stolen anything," commented Charlie.

"How would you know?" Grabowski demanded. "Someone could have taken some tetrodotoxin out of the tube."

"Impossible!" Charlie said immediately. "I wrote down every drop that we used. Then I added them up. The drops always matched the amount we started with."

"Someone could have added water to the tube after they took some out," Grabowski suggested. "After all, it looks like water."

Maxine looked at Charlie. "True," she admitted.

"Would you know from your experiments if you were using a weaker solution?" Grabowski asked.

"I'll check my records," said Maxine. "There might have been some unusual results. But results change for many reasons. The temperature of the room, for example."

Charlie added, "Or if Maxine took longer than three minutes to kill the rat and cut out the heart, that also changed the results."

Grabowski stared at Maxine. "You killed rats and cut out their hearts? And you timed yourself?"

"How else would I get a heart?" Maxine asked.

Grabowski continued to write in his notebook. "What happened to your tetrodotoxin when you stopped your research?"

Charlie answered. "We sent the tubes that we had not used back to the chemical supply company."

They walked back to the lab. "Do you still have all the records of your experiments?" Grabowski asked Charlie.

"Of course." He opened a drawer and gave Grabowski a pile of papers.

Grabowski looked quickly through the pages covered with numbers. Maxine looked over his shoulder.

"Do you have similar records?" Grabowski asked Maxine.

"Evidence, you mean?" she said. "Are you trying to connect me with Nanette's death?"

"I'm just doing my job," replied Grabowski. "That means I have to find out everything about this poison and how Nanette might have swallowed some."

"The records are at my house," Maxine said.

They went outside and walked to her car. Grabowski opened her car door. It was unlocked. He looked at her and shook his head. "Lock your car. Some day it'll get stolen."

Maxine said nothing but raised her eyebrows at him.

"This is a nice place to work," Grabowski commented. "Interesting research, nice lab, helpful lab assistant. Why did you leave?"

Maxine sighed. "I got divorced six months ago. I needed a change so I took a temporary job at Mercy Hospital ER."

"You left a successful career because you needed 'a change'? You didn't leave for other reasons?"

Maxine frowned. "What are you saying? That I left Marquette so I could poison Nanette and pretend the poison wasn't mine? Don't be silly. The poison may have come from my lab, but that doesn't mean I killed Nanette."

"She died in your ER from your research drug," said Grabowski. "In court, a lawyer could say that you knew she was poisoned and you chose to let her die."

"Why would I do that?" asked Maxine. "Remember it was me that asked for the autopsy. When the report said heart failure I asked Aaron to do more blood tests. I could have left the autopsy report as heart failure."

"What exactly is your relationship with Hank Myer?" Grabowski asked.

"Just friends." Maxine got into her car.

Grabowski sighed. The soft light of the street lamp showed the tired look on his face. "Maxine, today I learned that Hank Myer got a parking ticket the night of Nanette's burial. His car was parked in front of your house."

Maxine's face went red. "I'm not having an affair with Hank! I have never had an affair with Hank! That night, he slept on the couch. He came to my house because he was sad and lonely. He said he needed company."

"Not an intelligent thing to do," said Grabowski.

Maxine got angry. "Hank is a friend who needed help. And it's none of your business who stays in my house!" She shut her car door hard and drove away.

Chapter 6 *Grabowski gets no answers*

The next morning, Grabowski visited Hank's medical office to ask him some questions. The receptionist told him that Hank was a very busy doctor but he might have a few minutes to talk. She told him to take a seat.

Grabowski sat down feeling angry. He didn't like waiting. Also, he was already angry at Maxine and at himself. He liked Maxine a lot. They had gone out together once and he'd wanted to ask her out again. But he was so busy with his work, he hadn't had a chance yet. Now it looked like Maxine was having an affair with Hank. Maxine said she wasn't. But how could she let Hank stay overnight at her house only a few hours after Nanette's burial? What relationship did Maxine and Hank really have? And why did it matter to him so much?

At 9:30, the receptionist finally told Grabowski that Hank was ready to talk. Grabowski followed the receptionist down a hallway with paintings of flowers on the walls. Hank's elegant office had bookshelves on two walls, a thick Chinese rug, and long white curtains over the window.

Hank was sitting in a large leather chair behind a beautiful wooden desk. He looked cool and fashionable. Grabowski was wearing old trousers and a short-sleeved shirt that was damp with sweat. Grabowski sat down in a leather chair and looked at the paintings and Chinese rug. He wondered how much money Hank would get from Nanette's will.

"What can I do for you?" asked Hank. He looked tired.

"The police have discovered that your wife died from poison," said Grabowski. He was angry at having to wait half an hour. He didn't bother to tell Hank the news in a gentle way.

Hank looked shocked. "What are you talking about? Nanette died from heart failure. The autopsy report said that."

"Additional blood tests showed that the cause of Nanette's heart failure was a poison called tetrodotoxin," said Grabowski. He explained about tetrodotoxin. "We believe that Nanette swallowed the poison just before she died. Tetrodotoxin comes from the puffer fish."

"Fish! Nanette didn't eat fish!" Hank exclaimed. "She didn't like fish."

"We don't think she ate the fish. But somehow she swallowed the poison. What did Nanette do the day she died?" asked Grabowski.

"I don't know. I didn't see her. I left home very early that morning to go to the hospital. Then I drove to the station to catch the train to Chicago. I had a two-day conference at the Sheraton Hotel."

"Which train?" asked Grabowski.

"The eight thirty train. Why are you are asking these questions?" asked Hank.

Grabowski didn't answer. "You stayed at the Chicago Sheraton all day?"

"Yes, I was at the conference. After dinner, I went upstairs to my room. My receptionist called me there. She told me about Nanette."

"So you know nothing about what Nanette did that day," Grabowski repeated.

Hank rubbed his eyes. "She usually went to her classes at Marquette University. She was getting a degree in social work. Why was another blood test done?"

"An ER doctor asked for it." Grabowski said.

"Who?"

"Dr. Maxine Cassidy."

Hank looked surprised. "Maxine never told me that."

Grabowski ignored him. "I have more questions, if you don't mind. Who knew what Nanette did the day she died? Maybe some of the other students in her classes?"

"Maybe. I never met them. You can talk to her professors. Or her tennis coach at the Milwaukee Tennis Club."

"Your wife had two bottles of pills in her bag when she came to Mercy Hospital ER," said Grabowski. He read from his notebook. "Carisoprodol and Ferrous Sulphate. Your name is on the bottles as her doctor. Were you her doctor?"

"No," Hank answered. "She had her own doctor but when her medicine ran out, I wrote the prescription for more. It was easier for her. Why are you asking all these questions?"

"We think someone might have put the tetrodotoxin into her food or drink."

Hank's face turned pale. "You're saying that Nanette was murdered? That's why you're asking all these questions?"

"It's possible," said Grabowski.

"With poison from a fish? You're crazy!"

"We think the poison could have come from a research lab at Marquette. They used tetrodotoxin in experiments."

31

"Who did?" Hank demanded.

"Dr. Maxine Cassidy."

"Maxine? Impossible." Hank shook his head. "You said Maxine asked for the additional blood tests."

"I'm not saying that Maxine poisoned your wife. I'm saying that she used the poison in her lab experiments," corrected Grabowski.

Just then the receptionist knocked on the door and opened it. "Doctor, there are patients waiting for you," she said.

Hank stood up and looked at his watch. "I'm busy. If you have more questions, you'll have to come back."

"I do have more questions and I want the answers now. Why was your wife wearing such strange clothing when she died?" Grabowski asked.

Hank frowned. "What strange clothing?"

"The red wig. The black leather miniskirt."

"Nanette was wearing a leather miniskirt the night she died?" Hank asked, surprised.

"Yes. Do you know why?" Grabowski asked again.

Hank didn't answer. He opened the office door and started to leave.

"You don't seem very interested in Nanette's clothes and behavior. That's surprising," commented Grabowski. "Isn't it unusual for a woman from the richest part of Milwaukee to put on a leather skirt and spend her evening in a very rough neighborhood?"

But Hank had already hurried away. The next two hours were a waste of time. Grabowski phoned Nanette's doctor, but the doctor told Grabowski to get a court order if he wanted medical information about Nanette.

For the rest of the morning, Grabowski drove to the houses of the women who played tennis with Nanette. They were all wives of doctors and they all had sun-brown skin, strong arms and legs, and expensive clothes. Grabowski sat in their million-dollar houses and drank iced tea, but he got no answers to his questions. No-one knew what Nanette was doing in the rough neighborhood. No-one knew why she was wearing a black leather miniskirt and a red wig when she died.

By noon, Grabowski knew that Nanette played tennis three mornings a week and she played card games one evening a week. She was married once before in Chicago, but no-one knew her first husband. She had married Hank nine years before. They had no children. Nanette had worked as a model until two years before. Then she started studying at Marquette University for a social work degree.

Grabowski felt annoyed. If Nanette had a secret life, nobody knew about it. Or if they did know, they wouldn't tell him.

Chapter 7 *Hank gets angry*

At 2:00 PM Maxine was at home washing shampoo out of her hair when the doorbell rang. Grabowski? She put on a bathrobe and hurried to the door. But it wasn't Grabowski. It was another police officer who had come to pick up Maxine's research papers.

"Don't lose anything," said Maxine. "I'll need those papers when I go back to my research at Marquette in six months. Tell that to Grabowski."

That morning, Maxine had looked through these papers, looking for any unusual figures that might show that someone had added water to her tetrodotoxin solutions. She found nothing unusual.

After the police officer left, Maxine drove downtown to Marquette University. She needed to talk to someone about what was happening. She thought of Virginia Gaust. Virginia shared a lab with Maxine. If the poison that killed Nanette came from Maxine's lab refrigerator, Virginia might have an idea how that had happened.

Maxine parked her car under the same trees by the biochemistry building where she had parked it the night before. Inside was a strong smell of research chemicals used by students and professors. She knocked on Virginia's office door. Virginia was sitting at her desk staring at her computer. Papers covered her desk.

"Maxine," she called out with her usual good cheer. She quickly put her papers into her drawer. "I was just talking about you with a handsome police detective named Grabowski. He says that Nanette died from poison. He also said you asked for tests to be done for that poison. How did you know?"

"Stanley suggested it." Maxine took some exam papers off a chair and sat down. "What else did Grabowski ask you?"

"He asked how long I'd known you, what kind of researcher you were, how careful you were with your chemicals. What's going on, Maxine?"

Maxine decided to tell Virginia everything – except about Hank spending the night at her house after Nanette's burial. But before she could start explaining, she was interrupted by Charlie. He came in and sat down.

Virginia frowned at him. "Don't you have work to do?" she asked Charlie.

"It can wait," answered Charlie. "Are you talking about Nanette's murder?" he asked Maxine. "Does Grabowski have his eye on anyone besides us? Last night I thought he was going to put us both in jail."

Virginia was listening closely. "What did Grabowski tell you?" she asked.

"He said he hasn't found any other place in Milwaukee where there is tetrodotoxin – only this lab," Maxine replied.

"Maxine!" Virginia cried. "If Grabowski thinks the tetrodotoxin came from here, doesn't that put you in a bad position?"

"It puts me in big trouble, as Grabowski said. For that reason, I want to find out where Nanette got the poison – in case Grabowski decides I poisoned her."

Virginia frowned.

"That poison acts quickly," Maxine said. "Grabowski needs to find out who Nanette was with just before she came to Mercy Hospital."

"How did she get to Mercy Hospital?" asked Charlie.

"Taxi," answered Maxine.

Charlie smiled. "There's your answer. Find the taxi driver and ask where he picked her up."

Virginia turned to Charlie. "You waste a lot of time sitting around doing nothing! No wonder you don't have your Ph.D. yet!"

"I don't have my Ph.D. because you won't approve my reports," said Charlie angrily.

Maxine ignored the usual argument between Charlie and Virginia. They had never liked each other. "I'll ask Grabowski if he's found the taxi driver," Maxine said. She wrote a note for herself. She would ask Grabowski when she saw him again. She got up to leave.

Virginia held up a hand. "Do you want to play tennis at the club after work tomorrow night, Maxine?" she asked. "I'll be up until midnight too, working here. The tennis courts are always free after midnight."

Maxine agreed. She used to play with Virginia once a week at midnight at the tennis club. It stayed open all night.

Charlie followed Maxine to the entrance door of the building.

"Charlie," said Maxine. "What's wrong with Virginia? You two never got along, but she's getting even ruder. If you would put on a clean shirt and shave, she might be nicer."

Charlie looked around to make sure no-one heard him. "Virginia's been in a terrible mood lately. I think she's having trouble with her research."

"Impossible!" exclaimed Maxine. "Virginia's famous for her research. Research is her life – all she does is work."

Charlie shook his head. "This year, the Research Review Committee at Marquette will review her research. They'll decide whether she will keep her lab and office, her salary – everything. Even if the drug company keeps giving her money, she might not have a place to do her research."

"Virginia will have no problem getting her research approved," laughed Maxine.

Charlie lowered his voice. "She stopped doing any lab work months ago. She told me that she doesn't need the lab computer anymore. But she sits in her office for hours working on her reports – as if she is having trouble."

"Maybe she's writing something for a medical magazine," suggested Maxine.

Charlie lowered his voice. "I think her research money has been cut, Maxine. Six months ago, she said she would buy a new refrigerator for the lab using her research money. But we still have no new refrigerator."

"You and Virginia don't like each other, but that's no reason to doubt her research," frowned Maxine.

"This has nothing to do with me. Virginia has been seeing Hank. Lunches, dinners – for months. Hank is the head of the Research Review Committee."

"So?"

"I think Virginia is trying to persuade him to approve her research," Charlie said. "I think she knows it might not get approved."

"How do you know? Have you read her reports?" demanded Maxine.

But Charlie saw Virginia coming down the hall. He hurried away.

Back at Mercy Hospital, Maxine went to the pay phone in the hall to call Grabowski. She wanted to ask Grabowski where the taxi had picked up Nanette. She wanted to ask if he knew why Nanette had been wearing a black leather miniskirt the night she died. She also wanted to ask if Grabowski had found another place to get tetrodotoxin in Milwaukee.

Maxine called Grabowski's office. He was out so she left a message with the secretary. Maxine was worried. Why did Grabowski get so upset when he thought she was having an affair with Hank? Did Grabowski think that Hank had murdered Nanette? Worse, did Grabowski believe that Maxine had killed Nanette?

At 8:00 PM, Maxine went to the hospital cafeteria for dinner. At a small table in a quiet corner, she read her list of questions. She was thinking about what else she should ask Grabowski when a hand dropped on her shoulder. Hank sat down next to her. His lips were tight and his face was white.

"Detective Grabowski came into my office today with a crazy story. He said Nanette was poisoned. He said it might be murder!" Hank's blue eyes were like stones. "He said you gave him that idea."

"Hank, I should have called you. I wanted to wait until I knew more."

"Nanette is dead and buried. Can't you leave her alone?" Hank asked.

"A healthy young woman with no history of a heart problem drops dead of a heart attack. It isn't right."

"Why do you care, Maxine?"

"I'm trying to find out the truth. Hank, why does this bother you?"

"It bothers me because I don't want this dark shadow hanging over her," Hank said. "Nanette and I had our troubles, but I loved her."

"I'm sorry, Hank."

He put his face in his hands for a moment. "It's out of our hands now." He pushed back his chair.

Chapter 8   *Maxine and Grabowski talk*

The next morning, Maxine got up at 8:00 AM. She wasn't working until 3:00 PM, but it was such a beautiful summer morning with birds singing that she woke up early. Cool air from Lake Michigan blew through the trees outside her window. She pulled on her bathing suit with shorts and a T-shirt over it and put some sandwiches into the basket of her bicycle. Soon she was riding her bicycle toward Lake Michigan.

When she reached the lake, she took the bike path that went south along Lake Michigan. A few swimmers were in the lake, but Maxine decided to keep bicycling to a nicer beach half an hour further down.

Maxine was bicycling slowly and looking at the sailboats when she heard someone call her name. She looked around and saw Grabowski sitting on the front steps of a small house. He waved to her.

Surprised, Maxine stopped her bicycle. "I didn't know you lived here," she said. She wheeled her bicycle to his driveway and left it by his car.

"Want a coffee?" Grabowski asked. He walked into the house. Maxine followed.

"Just a glass of water would be great," she said.

The front room had a lovely stone fireplace but not much furniture. There was an old green couch, a big armchair with a blanket over the seat, and a TV sitting on a chair. The large kitchen had a nice round wooden table but the two chairs were old. Grabowski gave Maxine a glass of cold water.

They went back outside to sit on the front steps. Maxine looked at the blue lake. "It must be nice to live across the street from Lake Michigan. If I lived in this neighborhood, I'd swim in the lake all summer."

"When I bought this house, I hoped to find someone to share it with me." He looked at her. "When this is all over, let's take a long bicycle trip along the lake."

Maxine was surprised. "Does this invitation mean that you don't think I poisoned Nanette?"

"I never thought you did, Maxine, although I wish I could prove it."

"Let me help you. I can find things out that you can't," said Maxine. "The murder happened in my world. Nanette was a doctor's wife. A doctor – me – found the poison. The poison came from a medical research lab. Your only suspects are Hank and me – two doctors. I knew Nanette socially, and I know all the doctors who are connected to her. I can tie all these facts together for you."

Grabowski held his cold beer can against his face. "These doctors and their wives won't tell me anything," he admitted. "I'm wasting my time talking to them."

"There must be something we're overlooking," Maxine said. She was quiet for a moment. Finally she spoke, "Where did the taxi pick up Nanette to bring her to Mercy Hospital?"

"On the corner of North Avenue and 24th Street, a few blocks from Mercy Hospital," answered Grabowski.

"What was she doing?"

"Don't know. The taxi driver said she was alone," said Grabowski.

"Did anyone in that neighborhood see her?" Maxine asked.

"In that neighborhood nobody talks to police," Grabowski said.

"Don't you have plain-clothes police there?" Maxine asked.

"Yes, but they are looking for people selling drugs. None of the plain-clothes police saw Nanette or heard about her, which means she wasn't selling or buying drugs."

"That's good news," Maxine said. Then she frowned.

Grabowski touched her arm. "What is it?"

"Hank came to Mercy Hospital ER last night. He was angry that you are investigating Nanette's death. He was angry at me for asking questions."

"Why?" asked Grabowski. "Doesn't he want to know why she died?"

"I don't know. It's strange," Maxine said.

"Maybe he knows something that he doesn't want me to find out," said Grabowski.

Maxine didn't answer.

"Tell me about Virginia," Grabowski went on. "You worked with her in your lab at Marquette. What does she do at Marquette?"

"She teaches medical students and she does research that is world famous. Virginia has a brilliant career."

"You sound jealous," Grabowski said with a smile.

"No." Maxine shook her head. "Virginia has a brilliant mind. And she works harder than any researcher I know. She's at her lab nights, weekends, holidays. She also gets more money for her research than anyone I know."

"What is her research?" Grabowski asked.

Maxine didn't answer for a long time. "Can you keep this quiet? It's not a secret, but Virginia doesn't want it to become public information."

"Is she worried someone might steal her ideas?" Grabowski asked.

"No. People might get nervous. Virginia is trying to find a new drug to stop leprosy."

"Leprosy!" Grabowski looked shocked.

"Don't worry. Leprosy can be cured with antibiotics," Maxine explained. "It's a skin disease."

"Then why is Virginia looking for a new drug?"

"People with leprosy have to take three different antibiotics for one year," Maxine continued. "They take two different antibiotics once a month, and another antibiotic each day. The problem is that most leprosy cases are in poor countries where there are wars or drought. People often have to leave their homes and live in different places. It's difficult for doctors to find these people and give them all the pills for a year. It would be better to find a drug that cured leprosy more quickly and with fewer pills."

"What's the situation in the US?" Grabowski asked.

"Virginia told me that about 150 people get leprosy each year."

"Do you think Virginia will find a new drug?" Grabowski asked.

"She says she's making progress." Maxine didn't tell Grabowski what Charlie had said about Virginia's problem with her research. "But even if Virginia has found a new drug, it has to be approved by the Federal Drug

Administration, the FDA. This can take years. The leprosy disease only grows on humans and on mice feet. Experimenting on people is rarely allowed by the FDA so Virginia uses mice. She's hoping that the FDA will agree that if the drug works on mice, it will also work on people."

Grabowski nodded. "How does Virginia get money for her research?"

"From the federal government and from drug companies. They give the money to Marquette University. Then the University Research Review Committee decides how much money to give to Virginia. Hank is head of the Research Review Committee. Because her research is important, Virginia gets a lot of research money, plus a lab."

"What happens when her research doesn't go well?" asked Grabowski.

"The Research Review Committee might keep giving her money and wait until her results improve. But they might also give the money to someone else." Maxine finished drinking her water. "Why do you ask about Virginia?" she asked.

"The police have been checking everything Hank does. His car was parked outside Virginia's home several times since his wife died. All night."

"So?"

"He's on the Marquette University Research Review Committee," said Grabowski. "Should they be so friendly?"

"If her research is going well, it doesn't matter," said Maxine. She bicycled home a short time later and drove to Mercy Hospital. Her first patient was Lavelle.

Chapter 9 *Attack at the tennis club*

Lavelle had come back so Maxine could examine the cut on her arm. While Shirley was taking off the large bandage, Maxine noticed some white spots on Lavelle's arm. "Does this itch?" she asked.

Lavelle shook her head. "What happened to Mae West?" she asked. "I saw her here when I came with my cut arm."

"Mae West?"

"That isn't her real name." Lavelle smiled. "She told us to call her Mae West. You know, like the film star. She was a strange lady."

"Nobody came in here called Mae West," Shirley said.

"It was last week," Lavelle said. "Mae died. Too bad. She was a nice lady."

"Lavelle, are you talking about a woman with a red wig?" Maxine asked.

"That's right."

Shirley shook her head. "Her name wasn't Mae West."

"I told you her real name isn't Mae West," Lavelle said. "How did she die?"

Shirley looked at Maxine. "Is she talking about Nanette?"

"Lavelle, how do you know her name was Mae West?" Maxine asked.

"It's a long story," said Lavelle. She stood up. "I have to go. I'm late."

"I have to talk to you about this," Maxine said. "Can we meet tomorrow?"

Lavelle looked unsure for a moment and then said, "I can't tomorrow. I can meet you the day after. Café Italia. Across from the North Avenue Public Health Clinic. Around noon." Then she left.

At midnight, after work, Maxine drove to the Milwaukee Tennis Club. Only a few cars were parked in front of the club, but Virginia's wasn't there. Maxine wasn't surprised. Virginia was always late. The receptionist wasn't behind the counter, either. Probably she went to get coffee. The long hall to the dressing rooms was dark. Maxine walked to the women's dressing room and opened the door.

"Virginia?" she called, but the room was empty. She hung up her jacket and changed into her tennis dress. She was pulling her sweater over her head when she heard someone walking out of the shower room behind her.

"Virginia?" she called, turning around. But suddenly, the lights went out. The room was completely black. "Hey! Turn on the light!" she shouted. Behind her, she heard a noise.

"Who's there!" she called. She waited, listening for footsteps. She moved toward the door to the hall, quietly feeling along the wall to find the light switch. She heard someone breathing and the small sound of a footstep. Someone was in the room with her. "Help!" she shouted.

Suddenly, a blow came out of the dark. Something hit her over the back of the head.

"Help!" she screamed again, hoping the receptionist would hear. She fell forward over a chair, hitting her head against a cupboard with cans of tennis balls. The cans fell on the floor noisily. The noise told the attacker where she was. Another blow hit her on the head again, and on the arm.

"Stop!" she screamed. She fell on the floor, covering her head with her arms.

Just then, shouts came from the reception area. The door to the hallway opened and closed. The person had left.

Footsteps were coming down the hall toward the women's dressing room. When the door opened and the light went on, Maxine was lying on the floor, her head and arm covered with blood.

"Maxine!" Virginia gasped. A moment later, the receptionist and a security guard entered.

"Where were *you*?" Virginia asked them angrily. She knelt beside Maxine and looked at her head and arms. "Maxine, can you hear me? You're gonna be OK."

The security guard phoned for an ambulance. The receptionist looked shocked. "I only left the desk for a few minutes," she said quietly.

The ambulance took Maxine to Mercy Hospital. When the ambulance medics brought her into Mercy Hospital ER, Grabowski was waiting.

"How did you know I was coming in an ambulance?" Maxine groaned. She had trouble talking, her head hurt so much.

"The ambulance called the ER to say they were bringing you. Shirley called me." Grabowski held her hand. "What happened, Maxine?"

"Somebody came into the women's dressing room while I was waiting for Virginia and hit me over the head!"

"But why?" exclaimed Virginia, who had followed the ambulance in her car.

"The doctor is ready to see Maxine," Shirley said. "Talk to her later."

Maxine closed her eyes. She felt Grabowski's lips on her cheek. She woke up the next morning in a hospital bed. Her right arm didn't move. It was held tight with a bandage. Then she saw Grabowski sitting in a chair.

"The nurse said that you shouldn't move your fingers," he said. "How do you feel?"

"Terrible."

"What can you remember about the attack?" Grabowski asked.

"The light went off and someone hit me," Maxine said.

"Man or woman?"

"I don't know," Maxine replied. "Didn't the receptionist at the tennis club see someone go into the women's dressing room before me?"

Grabowski shook his head. "The receptionist was in the bathroom. Virginia came to the club a bit later. She was sorry she was late."

"I'm sorry too," said Maxine. She closed her eyes.

At noon, the doctor told Maxine she could go and Grabowski drove her home.

"Lock all your doors and go to bed. I'll come back this evening," Grabowski said.

At dinner time Maxine awoke and got out of bed. Grabowski was sitting at her kitchen table reading police reports. Maxine leaned against the wall, waiting for her legs to feel stronger. Grabowski looked up. His gray eyes got wide.

"Should you be out of bed?" he asked.

"I'm tired of bed." Maxine looked into the mirror over the sink. Her neck was purple and red next to the bandages. Her nose and chin had large red marks. And her arm was bandaged to the elbow.

"Have you learned anything more about what happened?" Maxine asked.

"No-one at the tennis club knows anything," he sighed.

"Grabowski, I think this attack is connected to Nanette."

"Because you were attacked after you started asking questions about why Nanette died?"

"Yes," Maxine replied. "I think the person who poisoned Nanette wants to stop me from asking any more questions."

Chapter 10 *A new suspect*

The next morning, Maxine felt much better. When she got up, Grabowski had already gone to work. She called Shirley. "I'm coming to work today. But before then, I'm going to Café Italia to talk to Lavelle. I want to know how Lavelle met Nanette."

"Be careful," warned Shirley.

"Don't worry. Café Italia is across the street from the Public Health Clinic. Dr. Kareena Singh is working there. If I have a problem, I'll go into the clinic."

"Should you be getting so involved? Why don't you leave the investigation to the police?" Shirley asked.

"I need to do this," said Maxine. "My life's in danger. I need answers to my questions."

Maxine drank a cup of coffee. She found her box of photographs and put several photos of Nanette in her purse to show Lavelle. She went out to her car, which was parked in front of her house. Grabowski had kindly driven it home for her.

Café Italia on North Avenue was the best Italian restaurant in Milwaukee and was always crowded even though it was in the inner city. Maxine parked her car on North Avenue and walked in. Lavelle was sitting at a table having lunch. Maxine sat down with her and ordered a salad.

Lavelle looked at Maxine's injured neck and arm. "What happened to you?"

"I was attacked at the tennis club," Maxine said.

"It sounds more dangerous than my neighborhood!" Lavelle replied with a smile.

"I think the attack on me had something to do with your Mae West. I'm trying to find out who killed her. Will you look at these photos? Tell me if this is Mae West."

Maxine gave Lavelle the photos. They were taken at the last party at Hank and Nanette's house. Nanette was wearing black pants and a black T-shirt. She had her arms around Aaron. At her side, Charlie was talking to Virginia.

Lavelle looked at the photos quickly. She nodded. "That's the lady."

"Where did you meet her?" Maxine asked.

"On North Avenue, about a month ago. She was walking around talking to people. She paid me a hundred dollars just to talk to me and walk around with me," Lavelle replied.

"Why was she talking to all these people?" Maxine asked.

But Lavelle didn't answer. She was looking behind Maxine. A tall man was standing there. Grabowski.

Grabowski sat down in the chair next to Maxine. "When you didn't answer the phone at your house, I called Shirley. She said this meeting was about Nanette. I told you to stop asking questions, Maxine. You might get hurt again."

Lavelle said to Grabowski, "I want to help this nice lady doctor. She takes good care of me. She's not doing anything wrong. She's just asking me a few questions about Mae West."

"Who's Mae West?" asked Grabowski.

"Nanette called herself Mae West," explained Maxine.

"She used to walk up and down North Avenue talking to people. Lavelle was with her."

"When did you find this out?" Grabowski frowned. "Why didn't you tell me?"

"Lavelle told me when she came into ER the night I was attacked in the tennis club." Maxine answered. "I just forgot to tell you."

"Please remember that I'm the detective," warned Grabowski. He turned to Lavelle. "How often did Nanette, I mean Mae West, walk along North Avenue wearing a tight leather miniskirt?" he asked finally.

"A couple of times a week," Lavelle said.

"What did she do?" he asked.

"Mae just walked with us and talked to us," Lavelle answered. "Asked us questions about life in the neighborhood. About life on the street. She said she was writing a book."

Maxine spoke carefully. "I think that Nanette came down to North Avenue to find out what it's like for women who live in rough parts of the community. She was getting a degree in social work, remember? There's a lot of crime in this area and a lot of criminals. Maybe she found out something that she wasn't supposed to know."

"What do you mean?" asked Grabowski.

"Nanette was a curious person, always asking questions," Maxine explained. "There are some pretty dangerous characters in this neighborhood. I don't think they would have liked being watched, and they certainly wouldn't want anyone to write about them in a book. Maybe Nanette found out something pretty big."

Grabowski took out his notebook and turned to Lavelle.

"All right. Tell me what happened when you were out on the street with Mae West."

"Mae just talked to people," replied Lavelle. "One man drove up in a car and wanted her to get in. She wouldn't. The man looked angry."

"What did the man look like?" Grabowski asked.

Lavelle shrugged. "White man. Dressed nice."

"Did she ever get pills from anybody?" asked Maxine.

"Pills?" Lavelle looked nervous. She didn't answer.

"Drugs," Grabowski, interrupted. "Did she ever buy drugs?"

"No sir. She didn't even drink," Lavelle replied. "When we were in a bar, she had a club soda. But she was interested in the drug-taking that goes on around here. She wanted to write all about that in her book."

"Did she usually stay with you all evening?" Grabowski asked.

"Only a few hours. She wore high heels and when her feet started to hurt, she would drive away in her car. She put on a long red dress over her clothes," Lavelle added.

"Did she ever see that man again? The man who wanted her to get in his car?" Grabowski asked.

"No," Lavelle shook her head. "But a few days later, a different man stopped to talk to her. She got in the car with him and talked. Then they drove away together."

"What time was that?" Grabowski asked.

"About ten at night," Lavelle answered. "A couple of hours before she got sick."

"Sick?" Maxine cut in.

"When she went to the hospital to see you," Lavelle

explained. "That was the same night I saw her at Mercy Hospital ER."

Maxine picked up a photo of Nanette. "I wish I knew who she drove away with on the night she died."

"I can tell you that," Lavelle said. She picked up a photo from the table and put her finger right on the man in the middle.

"Aaron!" exclaimed Maxine.

Chapter 11 *Lies*

Lavelle left, and Maxine and Grabowski ordered coffee.

Maxine said to Grabowski, "I know what you're going to say. I should have told you I was meeting Lavelle for lunch. I should have told you about Mae West. But I wanted to talk to Lavelle on my own first. I wanted to find out as much as I could before I spoke to you."

"Maxine," said Grabowski, taking her hands. "I know you're not afraid to ask questions. I know you're a smart and determined woman. But finding out how Nanette died isn't your job. That's my job. I think Nanette was murdered, and I think you're in danger. From now on, please tell me any information you get and I'll take it from there."

"OK, OK," said Maxine. "But the important thing is that we now know Aaron was with Nanette the night she died! He can tell us why Nanette was on North Avenue."

Grabowski frowned. "Why didn't Aaron tell me this before? This is very suspicious. Maybe Aaron was the last person to see Nanette before she was poisoned."

Maxine gasped. "You think maybe Aaron poisoned Nanette? Why? He hardly knew her!"

They were both silent for a moment and then Maxine spoke. "Aaron did warn me not to ask for another blood test. He said I would find out things I might not want to know. But I can't believe he's a killer."

"Hank didn't want you to ask questions either," said

Grabowski. "Maybe both of them know something they don't want the police to know."

"Hank wouldn't poison Nanette," Maxine said in surprise. "He loved her!"

"How do you know he loved her? He came to your house the night after Nanette's burial. That makes it look like he wasn't very sad about losing his wife! He's been staying at Virginia's house too!"

"Next you'll be saying that Virginia poisoned Nanette!" Maxine said angrily.

Grabowski finished his coffee and stood up. "You learned that Nanette was calling herself Mae West. That night, somebody attacked you at the tennis club. Maybe there's a connection."

He and Maxine went out of the café to the hot street. "What do we do now?" Maxine asked. "Talk to Aaron?"

"*We* talk to no-one," Grabowski said. He took her arm and pulled her toward her car. "*I* talk to Aaron. You go to work."

"It's only two o'clock. I have an hour before I have to be at the hospital."

"Then go home and put some ice on your neck. You're turning purple," Grabowski said with a smile as he left.

Maxine sat in her hot car. An hour and nothing to do. Working in the ER had taught her to take action. Now she couldn't spend even a minute just waiting. The North Avenue Public Health Clinic was across the street. The public health doctor, Dr. Kareena Singh, took care of people in this neighborhood. She might have heard something about Nanette. Maxine got out of her car again.

Inside the clinic, it was cool. Dr. Singh was in her office talking to a nurse.

Dr. Singh pulled out a chair for Maxine and said, "One of the nurses just told me some strange news about how Hank Myer's wife died. They think she was poisoned?"

"What else did she hear?" asked Maxine. She sat down.

"That you used the same poison in your research; that you were working in Mercy Hospital ER when Nanette came in; that Nanette was wearing a leather miniskirt and a red wig," Dr. Singh said.

"All true," Maxine nodded.

"Why would anyone poison Nanette?" Dr. Singh asked.

"That's what I've been trying to find out," Maxine answered.

Dr. Singh smiled. "Aren't the police doing that?"

"Detective Grabowski is on the case, but I think he's looking in the wrong place. That poison acts quickly. Nanette had to have been poisoned while she was near Mercy Hospital."

Dr. Singh raised her eyebrows. "What was Nanette doing in that area?"

Maxine spoke quietly. "Did a woman called Mae West ever come in here?"

"Yes," answered Dr. Singh. "Early evening. I remember her because the nurses joked about her name, Mae West."

"Why did she come in?"

"Injured knee," Dr. Singh said. "She was wearing high heels and she fell on the sidewalk. Why?"

"That was Nanette," Maxine answered.

"You're joking."

"She said she was writing about life on North Avenue for

her university degree in social work," continued Maxine. "She was wearing those clothes and that wig the night she died. The taxi that brought her to Mercy Hospital stopped for her near here, on the corner of 24th and North Avenue. I just wish I knew what she was doing there the night she died."

At 2:30 PM Maxine said goodbye and walked down North Avenue to 24th Street. She stood where the taxi driver had picked up Nanette. A closed grocery was on one corner. An empty store was on another corner. On the third corner was an old apartment block with broken windows. It looked like no-one lived in it. The fourth corner had no buildings. Maxine looked through the window of the grocery. Nothing unusual.

It was nearly 3:00 PM when she got to Mercy Hospital. She hurried into the ER, saw that it was empty, and ran down the steps to the pathology lab. She wanted to ask Aaron if he had talked to Grabowski yet. The doors to the lab were locked. Maxine saw light under the door. She knocked loudly on the door.

"Aaron, it's me, Maxine. Let me in," she shouted.

After a minute, Aaron unlocked the door.

"Can't I work in peace?" he demanded. His eyes were red and he needed a shave. "I have so many bodies in here. I've got so much to do."

"Then you haven't talked to Detective Grabowski yet."

"Who?" He picked up a knife.

"The detective who came here a few days ago with Nanette's blood test results."

"I haven't told anyone I'm here today," Aaron said. "I need to get this work done. Say, what happened to you?"

He saw the bruises on her neck.

"I was at the tennis club and somebody attacked me when I was in the women's dressing room," Maxine said. "Hadn't you heard? It's all over the hospital."

"I haven't spoken to anyone in days. Who attacked you?"

"I don't know," Maxine said. "But I think I was attacked because I have learned something about Nanette's killer. The person is trying to stop me from knowing the truth."

"What have you learned?" Aaron picked up a new knife.

Maxine spoke quietly but clearly. "I learned that Nanette used to put on a tight leather skirt and a red wig and walk around on North Avenue. And I learned that you met Nanette on North Avenue and she got into your car."

The knife fell out of Aaron's hand.

"Aaron, tell me what happened to Nanette that night," Maxine demanded.

Aaron looked at his hand. The falling knife had cut his finger. He pulled off his gloves and threw them into the garbage.

"I don't know. I wasn't there." He started to wash his cut.

"But a woman who lives on North Avenue recognized you. She saw your photo," Maxine argued.

Aaron looked at Maxine. "What photo? Where did she get it?"

"I showed it to her. Aaron, did you meet Nanette on North Avenue?" Maxine insisted.

"I did not. I didn't know Nanette was walking around on North Avenue and I didn't meet her there."

"You're lying!" But Maxine's argument was cut off by her pager calling her to the ER. She hurried out.

Chapter 12 *Another attack*

At 11:45 PM, the ER was empty. Maxine felt exhausted. Shirley told her to go straight to bed. Maxine drove home with the windows open to let the soft night air cool her face. The cool wind made her feel more awake. As she drove into her neighborhood, the air became fresher with the smell of flowers and grass. A few streets from her house, she pulled into an all-night grocery for milk and bread.

As she got back into her car, she saw the dark figure in the back seat a second before a belt came around her neck and was pulled tight. Maxine couldn't breathe. She tried to get the belt from around her neck and as she did, her elbow hit the horn. The loud noise made the attacker let the belt loosen slightly. Maxine got her fingers under the belt, and leaned forward to push hard on the horn with her elbow. A young man coming out of the grocery heard the noise and ran over to the car. The attacker in the back seat jumped out and ran away.

The man drove her back to Mercy Hospital ER. Shirley was still there. She called Grabowski who arrived in fifteen minutes and began questioning the man who had helped Maxine. The young man said that the attacker was wearing dark clothes, black gloves, and a black cap. He couldn't say for certain if it was a man or a woman.

Once he had finished with the man, Grabowski went to see Maxine. His hand shook as he held her shoulder.

"I should have driven you home, Maxine. After one

attack, I knew this might happen. I'll never forgive myself."

"Not your fault, Grabowski." She felt sick. Her mouth was dry, her tongue felt too big, and her throat hurt too much to talk. She reached for Grabowski's hand and held it tightly. Soon afterwards, the nurse came to take her to a private room where she fell asleep.

When she awoke, Grabowski was sitting by her bed. Next to him was a vase of flowers.

"You shouldn't have!" Maxine smiled.

"I didn't. These are from your friends in the ER. These are from me." He handed her some tiny pink roses. He pulled out a notebook. "I want to find out why the attacker was hiding in your car last night. Did you do something yesterday to make the attacker nervous? Tell me what you did after I left you at Café Italia yesterday afternoon."

"OK. But don't get angry with me." Maxine told him about meeting Dr. Singh.

"I'll go and talk to Dr. Singh today," said Grabwski. "Maybe she'll remember something about Mae West that might help us."

"Have you found the taxi driver who picked up Nanette yet?" Maxine asked.

"Yes. I spoke to him earlier today," replied Grabowski. "He said Nanette was on the corner of 24th Street and North Avenue leaning against the wall next to a doorway. She was holding her stomach. When she saw the taxi driver she started waving her arms."

"I walked to the corner of 24th Street and North Avenue and looked around," Maxine said. "Have you been there?"

"Yes," said Grabowski. "There's nothing but empty

buildings and stores around there. I've asked one of our plain-clothes police officers to watch the corner."

"I talked to Aaron after I talked to Dr. Singh," Maxine said. "Aaron said he didn't go to North Avenue. He said he never saw Nanette. He's lying, but I don't know why."

Grabowski frowned. "Aaron could have killed her. You told Aaron that you knew he'd picked up Nanette a few hours before she died and that night you're attacked."

"Aaron couldn't have!" Maxine said.

"I'll decide that when I find him. He isn't at home. The hospital receptionist says he hasn't been there for two days."

"He's hiding in his lab," said Maxine. "He locks the door when he gets behind with his work and he doesn't tell the receptionist he is there."

Grabowski left to find Aaron. Maxine slept.

Hank stopped by at noon when he came to Mercy Hospital to see a patient. He kissed Maxine on the cheek. "It isn't safe for a single woman to work nights and go home to an empty house. Why don't you go back to Marquette University?"

"I'm being attacked because of Nanette's death, Hank. I know something that someone doesn't want me to know. If only I knew what it was."

Hank stood up angrily. "You're a doctor, not a detective. If the police can't find out the truth, how can you?"

"But I'm making someone nervous," Maxine went on. "I'm getting close."

"Nanette is dead. Leave her in peace now." He went out before she could answer.

Chapter 13 *Lavelle knows more*

Maxine slept for most of the day. At 6:00 PM. Grabowski arrived to take her home. She got in the car and closed her eyes. After a few minutes, she opened them to see Lake Michigan in front of her. Grabowski was parking in front of his house.

"What are we doing at your house?" asked Maxine.

"You're staying here until we find this killer. I want to keep an eye on you."

"Do you give this protection to all women who are attacked?" Maxine smiled at him.

"Only you." Grabowski smiled back.

"Thanks for taking care of me." He helped her into the house and she fell fast asleep on his bed.

The next morning, Maxine awoke early and found Grabowski sitting outside reading the newspaper and drinking coffee. He was wearing purple swimming trunks and a T-shirt.

Maxine looked at the blue waters of Lake Michigan. "What a beautiful spot for breakfast. I wish I felt strong enough for a swim."

Grabowski smiled. "You can come back any morning you want."

Maxine smiled at him. She sat down on the steps. "What happened while I was asleep? Did you find Aaron?"

"Yes," replied Grabowski.

"Did he admit that he met Nanette on North Avenue?" asked Maxine.

"Yes. He decided that it was better to tell the truth to police. But his story has a problem. He said he drove her home."

"Home!" said Maxine. "But she was on North Avenue when she got into the taxi."

Grabowski nodded. "Aaron says he doesn't know how she got back to North Avenue. But I think he's lying. Maxine, Aaron knew Nanette very well. He told me they were having an affair."

Maxine looked surprised and went quiet for a few moments. "Aaron found out that Nanette was walking around North Avenue. He loved her and felt responsible for her. He made her come home."

"You don't know how Aaron felt about her," Grabowski said. "Maybe he wanted to end the affair and she wouldn't let him. Maybe she was driving him crazy."

"That's not a reason for murder. Besides, where did he get the poison?"

"You've known him for years," Grabowski continued. "You must have talked about your research. He must have visited you at your lab and somehow stole the drug. He could have put it in a piece of candy or something."

"So you think Aaron attacked me at the tennis club and in my car?"

Grabowski shrugged. "Well, no-one knows where he was during those hours. I can't prove any of this, but I'm watching him." He stretched and stood up. "I'm going for a swim."

Birds flew over the beach. Maxine drank her coffee and

watched Grabowski swim in the cold water of Lake Michigan. Maxine tried to think. What did she know that was making the murderer of Nanette nervous? Maybe Nanette had said something important in the ER before she died.

She thought about the night Nanette died. Nanette had said she had never felt sick like this before. She had said she took a pill, whatever that meant.

A car stopped in front of the house. Hank got out.

"How did you find me?" Maxine asked.

Hank sat down on the steps next to her "Everybody at Mercy Hospital knows you are here. I hear Grabowski thinks Aaron killed Nanette."

"Grabowski's a detective," Maxine said. "It's his job to suspect everyone. And Aaron does look pretty suspicious at the moment. Did he tell you that he knew Nanette was walking around in the inner city at night? Did he tell you he saw her the night she died?"

"Yes. Maxine, he didn't kill her. I'm sure. He couldn't have."

"Hank, tell me the truth. Did you know that Nanette was walking around North Avenue?" Maxine asked.

Hank nodded. "I found out about a month ago. I phoned home several nights when I was working late. Nanette wasn't home. She wasn't with any of our friends. So I paid a private detective to follow her. He said she went to North Avenue to get information for her university degree. He said she watched the street life."

"Hank, why didn't you tell Grabowski that you knew where Nanette was on the night she died?"

"I didn't know where she was," answered Hank. "I was

in Chicago. But I figured it out when Grabowski told me she was wearing those terrible clothes. I didn't tell Grabowski because I didn't think her research on North Avenue was connected to her death."

"But you should have told Grabowski. He still suspects everyone. He even thinks you could have killed her."

"Me! Why?" Hank said in surprise.

"Because you came to my house after she died and you stayed all night. Grabowski thinks that shows that you didn't care about her. That you cared about me."

"Grabowski knows about that?" Hank frowned, worried.

"You parked your car on the wrong side of the street and the street cleaner called the police. Remember? You got a parking ticket."

"Then Grabowski must also think you had a reason to kill her," said Hank, angrily. "You could have got the poison." He sighed. "I wish you hadn't started this investigation, Maxine. My friends and colleagues don't like having police come to their homes and asking them personal questions. I don't like it either." He got in his car and drove away.

As he drove away, Grabowski came back from his swim. "What did Hank want?"

"I'm not sure. He told me he paid a private detective to follow Nanette. So he knew that Nanette was going there."

Grabowski wasn't surprised. "Lavelle said that Nanette talked to two men. One man just talked to her while Lavelle was there. The second man drove her away in his car the night she died. That was Aaron."

"Maybe Hank was the first man," Maxine suggested. "Why don't you ask Hank if he talked to Nanette when she was on North Avenue. Also I can show photos of Hank to Lavelle. Let's go and get them. They're in my house."

"Good idea," said Grabowski. "But I go alone. You stay here. And keep the door locked."

When Grabowski got back, he sat down with Maxine and looked at the photos. There were photos of Hank talking to Virginia. Charlie was standing behind them. Aaron and Kareena were eating.

On Tuesday afternoon, Maxine went back to work at Mercy Hospital ER. She still had bruises on her neck and now her right arm was bandaged from wrist to elbow, but she could use both her hands. The ER doors opened and the first patient of the night was Lavelle. She had fallen again and cut her arm even more badly than before.

"I'm going home to Alabama," Lavelle said. "I'm tired of Milwaukee. I've got about ten thousand dollars in the bank. I'm going to buy a house near my mother. A friend will drive me tonight. We'll get there in two days."

"Where did you get ten thousand dollars, honey?" Shirley asked.

Lavelle didn't answer. Shirley washed Lavelle's arm and Maxine started to work on the cut. She noticed the pale spots on Lavelle's arm again. "Lavelle, when did you get these spots?" she asked.

Lavelle shrugged.

Maxine walked outside with Lavelle to wait for her friend to pick her up. "Before you go," said Maxine, "Could you look at these other photos? Tell me if you saw this man?" She showed her the photos she took at the last party.

Lavelle pointed to Hank. "That's the man who talked to

her first, a few days before she died. He was the one that drove away."

"Thanks," said Maxine.

Lavelle's friend drove up and Lavelle got into the car. Lavelle leaned out the window. "The police don't really think you killed Mae West, do they?" Lavelle asked Maxine.

Maxine frowned. "The police are watching several people besides me. The problem is we don't know why anyone would want to kill Nanette. So the police are watching people who knew about that poison and had the chance to poison Nanette. And that includes me."

Lavelle spoke quietly. "The night Mae West died, she may have met somebody else. If she did, then that might be why she died."

"Who is this person?" demanded Maxine.

"I don't know the name. I shouldn't be saying any of this. I could get into trouble." Lavelle looked nervous. "It's someone in the photo you showed me. And go to North Avenue and 24th Street," she whispered, as the car moved away.

"Wait! Lavelle! North Avenue and 24th is where the taxi picked up Mae West. I've been there. There are only old houses and empty stores."

But the car was already out of sight.

Chapter 14   *Maxine investigates*

Grabowski came to the hospital at 9:00 PM to take Maxine to his house.

"Do you really think it's still necessary for me to stay with you?" asked Maxine, as Grabowski drove south on Lake Shore Drive. "If I go home, I promise to lock the doors of my house and my car from now on."

"I think that the person who killed Nanette is worried about what you know," said Grabowski. "You can either stay with me, or I can put a police guard in your house."

"I'd much rather stay with you," she said as the car stopped in front of Grabowski's house. It was a beautiful night. The stars were bright and the moonlight made a silver path across Lake Michigan to their feet. Maxine sat down and looked at the lake. Grabowski brought her a cold beer and sat down next to her.

"I saw Lavelle today," Maxine said. "She came into the ER."

"Did you show her the photos?" asked Grabowski.

"Yes," replied Maxine. "She pointed to Hank as the man who spoke to Nanette."

Grabowski didn't look surprised. "I thought so. Hank hired a private detective to follow Nanette once. He probably hated what Nanette was doing. Maybe he killed her because he felt embarrassed by her."

"You can't prove any of this, Grabowski."

"Maxine, in a murder case, I ask questions, I collect information, then I form a theory and try to prove it."

"I do the same in research," Maxine said. "But the information I collect depends on the questions I ask. If I ask the wrong question, I get the wrong information. I develop the wrong theory. You're asking the wrong questions."

Grabowski sighed. "I don't even know why someone wanted Nanette dead."

Maxine pulled out the photo in her purse. "Lavelle told me this evening that Nanette might have met someone else at the corner of 24th Street and North that night. She told me to look at this photo – the one at the party with everyone in it."

Grabowski looked at the photo. "This doesn't help. We already know all these people. We can't find any unusual connection to Nanette. And all we know is that on the night Nanette died, Aaron says he took her home."

"Now we have to find out how Nanette got back to North Avenue after Aaron took her home. Her car was still on North Avenue, remember," Maxine said.

Grabowski sighed. "You believe Aaron. I don't. I talked to the taxi companies. No taxis picked up a woman wearing a red wig from the East Side and took her to North Avenue. The only taxi driver took her to Mercy Hospital."

"Maybe she took a bus?"

"No. We talked to the bus drivers on that route. It was late at night. They would have remembered her. Maxine, we have a witness who saw Aaron pick up Nanette that night – Lavelle. I need to talk to her."

Maxine shook her head. "You can't. Tonight Lavelle went home to Alabama."

"What!" Grabowski shouted. "Why didn't you tell me?"

"I only found out tonight. She's tired of Milwaukee. She'll get to Alabama in about two days."

Grabowski sat back in his chair. "Lavelle suddenly decides she's tired of Milwaukee? More likely that Aaron made her leave. So our only witness has gone. He probably paid for her trip."

"Aaran wouldn't do that. Though I did wonder where she got her money from."

"Exactly," said Grabowski. "She lives in the roughest part of Milwaukee and suddenly she has money for a new life in Alabama?"

"I'm sure Aaron didn't kill Nanette, Grabowski," Maxine insisted. "And how could he even know Lavelle?"

Grabowski put his arm around Maxine and smiled at her. Surprised and a little confused, Maxine returned the smile. Then, inside the house, the phone rang.

Grabowski went in to answer it. He shouted into the phone and came out, banging the door. "I have to go downtown. A problem with another case. I don't want you to stay here alone. I'll call a police officer to stay with you."

"Don't be silly. I'll be fine," Maxine said.

"I worry about you. Everybody at Mercy Hospital knows where you are. I want you to go inside and lock the door. Open it only for me." He squeezed her hand and left the house.

Maxine watched the tail lights of his car go around the corner. She felt confused but oddly comforted when she was with Grabowski. She suddenly realized she liked him a lot. She hoped she would see more of him when this case was over.

She started thinking about all the people involved. She started thinking about Virginia. Maxine had known Virginia for three years at Marquette. They used to discuss their research for hours. Charlie had said Virginia was having trouble with her research. Maxine hadn't called her for a long time to talk. She went inside and called Virginia's home number. No answer. She tried the lab. Charlie answered.

"Virginia went out to dinner with Hank at 8:00 PM. She should be back any time now," he said.

Maxine hung up. It was already after 10:00 PM. Virginia should be back in the lab soon and could talk. Maxine called a cab to take her back home so she could get her car. Then she drove downtown.

Charlie was in his lab. He jumped when Maxine opened the door. "Maxine! What are you doing here? You're hurt! What happened?"

"It's a long story, Charlie, all about Nanette. The person who killed her thinks I know more than I do." Maxine sat down.

"And you drove here alone late at night? Are you crazy?" Charlie demanded, shocked.

"Listen, Charlie. Just before Nanette died, she went somewhere. We don't know where. This may be the key to the whole mystery. Aaron says he picked her up on North Avenue at 10:00 PM on Sunday night and took her home. We know she was back on North Avenue at 11:40 PM. How did she get back there? Grabowski has asked taxi drivers and bus drivers, but none of them remember her."

Charlie was staring at her, his eyes wide. "Nanette died Sunday night?"

"Didn't you know?"

"No! The burial was Wednesday. I never knew what day she died."

"Why is it important?" Maxine asked.

"Nanette phoned me here on Sunday night," Charlie explained. "I was working late. She was at home. She said she needed a ride to her car. She had left it on North Avenue."

"You know Nanette that well?" Maxine was surprised.

Charlie's face turned red. "I went to her last party, remember? I met her a month before that. Nanette came to the lab one day to talk to Virginia. Virginia wasn't here. Nanette asked me a lot of questions about the equipment and the experiments I was doing for Virginia. She came back three or four times. She was nice to me. We got along well."

"So when she called you on Sunday night, you picked her up?" Maxine asked.

"That's right. She said Hank was out of town and her friends were asleep."

"Couldn't she wait until morning?" Maxine asked

"She said she needed to drive to the university early the next morning," Charlie replied. "So I drove to her house. She was waiting outside for me. I drove her to her car."

"That's great!" Maxine felt happy. "This means that Aaron did bring Nanette home. This means that Aaron wasn't the last person to see Nanette before she was poisoned. You were!"

Charlie looked shocked. "Oh no! Now this looks bad for

me. The police might think I killed her. But I didn't. I just gave her a ride. You believe me, don't you Maxine?"

"I believe you, Charlie. But we have to find the person who saw her after you did." Maxine started to go out the door.

"Wait!" said Charlie. "I didn't tell you what I found in Virginia's desk."

Maxine felt very tired. She wanted to go to bed. "Charlie, don't tell me about your fight with Virginia. It's not my business. Even if Virginia is lying to the university about her research and if she is having trouble with money, what can I do?"

"You've been Virginia's friend, for years," Charlie said. "Maybe you can help her. Maybe if you looked at her reports again, you'd understand what to do."

"All right," said Maxine. "Where are these reports?"

Charlie took a big envelope from his desk. "Here they are. I took them from her office when she went out tonight. I was right. Virginia is in big trouble. These reports show that she isn't close to finding a new drug for leprosy."

Maxine frowned. She picked up a letter from the file. "That doesn't make sense. This is a copy of a letter that Virginia wrote to the university and the drug company. Virginia says that she has discovered a new leprosy drug and she wants permission from the FDA to test it on humans."

"Strange!" Charlie shook his head. "These reports don't show good results, even on mice. The Federal Drug Administration would never allow her to test her drug on people."

"Maybe Virginia is lying about her research to the FDA, the drug company, and to the university!" said Maxine.

"That's what I've been telling you," nodded Charlie. "Virginia would lie rather than lose her research money and her position at the university."

"I need to talk to Virginia about this," said Maxine.

Charlie looked at his watch. "She should be back by now. Maybe she isn't coming back tonight. Maybe she's with Hank." His face turned red. "Maybe you should wait until morning to talk to her."

Maxine frowned. She wouldn't be able to sleep if she went home now. Lavelle had told her to go to the corner of 24th Street and North Avenue. She decided to go there. Maybe there would be something there at night that wasn't there during the day.

Chapter 15 *24th Street and North Avenue*

Maxine drove down North Avenue and parked on 24th Street by the grocery. She noticed the doorway by the side of the grocery that the taxi driver had said Nanette was standing by. She decided to investigate.

Maxine went through the doorway and up the stairs. At the top of the stairs there was just an empty room. Disappointed, she came back down, but as she came out of the doorway she saw two women walking toward her. They stopped and looked at Maxine suspiciously.

"Can you help me?" Maxine asked. "I'm looking for a place that Lavelle told me about."

The women looked at each other and then back at Maxine. "How do you know Lavelle?" one asked.

"I'm her doctor at Mercy Hospital."

The women looked at each other. "Lavelle isn't here," one said.

"I know. She went to Alabama. Lavelle told me to come to 24th Street and North Avenue. She didn't say which house," Maxine answered.

One woman pointed to the grocery. "It's up those stairs. Nobody's there now. Wait a few days."

"I don't want to wait," answered Maxine.

"There's a phone number you can call. I have the phone number at home. Call me tomorrow. After noon." She gave Maxine her telephone number. Maxine hurried to her car to write it down.

By the time Maxine got back to Grabowski's house, her eyes were heavy with sleep. Grabowski's car was parked in the garage. She opened the kitchen door slowly. Grabowski was asleep on the sofa.

When she woke the next morning, Grabowski had left for work. A note lay under the coffeepot. Grabowski wrote that he would phone at noon. If she didn't answer, he would find her and arrest her for her own safety.

At 12:00 PM, Maxine phoned the woman she met on 24th and North Avenue the night before. She wanted to get the phone number the woman had told her about. The phone rang ten times. No answer. Maxine got some coffee and sat down to think. First, Charlie had said that he brought Nanette back to North Avenue. That meant that Charlie saw Nanette after Aaron did. But who saw Nanette after Charlie?

Maxine was also worried about Virginia and wanted to talk to her about her research. Virginia had to stop lying to the drug company and the university. She could ruin herself. She called Virginia's office, but there was no answer. Before she could call Virginia at home, Grabowski phoned.

"Where did you go last night?" he demanded.

"I went to the university to talk to Charlie. I found out some very important information. Charlie saw Nanette after Aaron did. Charlie drove Nanette from her home back to North Avenue. Now we know that Aaron didn't kill Nanette!"

"Why didn't Charlie tell us this before?" Grabowski asked.

"We didn't ask the right question. Charlie didn't know we were talking about Sunday night."

Grabowski sighed. "Good work, Maxine. But please stop driving around in the middle of the night. You've already been attacked. I want you to stay at my house today until you drive to Mercy Hospital. I'll come to the ER tonight and follow you home. Don't leave the ER without me."

Maxine hung up the phone. She wanted to talk to Virginia. She could drive to Virginia's house on her way to Mercy Hospital. She called Virginia at home.

Virginia answered right away. "Come over, Maxine," she said. "I need to talk to you."

Virginia lived in a large brick house with a beautiful garden. A stone wall around the garden had pots of flowers on it. Her house was only a few blocks from Maxine's house. Maxine rang the doorbell, but Virginia did not come to the door.

"Virginia!" Maxine called, but there was no answer. She walked around the house. She knocked on the back door. "Virginia!" she shouted, but there was no answer.

Maxine went to the garage to look for Virginia's car. The garage was near the back door. Virginia's car was in the garage with the engine running. There was a strong smell of gasoline.

"Virginia!" Maxine shouted. "Help! Somebody call an ambulance!" she screamed in the direction of the street. She put a handkerchief over her mouth and nose and ran into the garage. Behind her, a shadow moved. She turned to see who it was. Then something hit her on the head. Everything went black.

When she woke up, she was in an ambulance. There was another person lying next to her in the ambulance: Virginia. Virginia had also been hit on the head. The ambulance driver told Maxine that the neighbors had heard her screams. The neighbors had called the ambulance and the police.

When they got to Mercy Hospital ER, Virginia and Maxine were sent to surgery. She got out of surgery two hours later. Grabowski was waiting for her.

"I told you to go straight to work, Maxine!" Grabowski's face was pale. "Why didn't you ask me to come with you to Virginia's house?"

"I wanted to talk to Virginia about her research," Maxine said. "She wouldn't have talked about it with a police officer sitting there. Where is Virginia?"

"Home. She had a cut on the head, but it wasn't serious."

"I have to talk to her," said Maxine.

Grabowski shook his head. "A crazy person is following you. Promise me you will stay here until I take you home."

Grabowski went out in the hall. He met Hank coming out of the elevator. Hank looked worried.

"How's Maxine?" he asked. "What happened to her?"

"She was attacked again. This time at Virginia's house. Virginia was also attacked," answered Grabowski.

"It's because of this stupid investigation!" said Hank. "I told Maxine to stop. I told her she would get in trouble."

"Where have you been?" demanded Grabowski. "I tried to reach you at 1:00 PM today. Your receptionist said you had just left. She didn't know where you were. Your cell phone was turned off."

Hank looked nervous. "Aaron called me. We got some sandwiches and ate them in a park near my office. Aaron wanted to talk about Nanette. Aaron thought I didn't know that Nanette had been going to North Avenue. He thought I didn't know that he was having an affair with her. But I did know – I paid a private detective to follow her."

Hank's pager beeped. He looked at his watch. "I'm busy. Talk to me later."

Grabowski held up his hand. "An hour ago, I arrested Aaron for the murder of Nanette."

"No!" said Hank. "You've made a mistake!"

"We found out that Aaron's car was parked three blocks from Virginia's house at lunchtime. He had time to hit Virginia on the head, turn on the car engine, and then hit Maxine before he met you for lunch."

Chapter 16 *Hank takes action*

Maxine sat in her hospital room, unable to sleep or even rest. She didn't want to stay in the hospital, but the surgeon said she should stay at least one night. She kept thinking about Nanette. Hank walked into her room and sat down in the chair. He looked very tired.

"Grabowski has arrested Aaron. I just spent three hours at the jail, getting a lawyer for Aaron to get him out. I know Aaron didn't kill Nanette," he said.

"Grabowski has made a big mistake!" Maxine exclaimed.

"Grabowski says that the police saw Aaron's car a few blocks from Virginia's house at the same time that someone attacked you and Virginia in Virginia's garage. The truth was that Aaron was parked in front of your house. He was waiting for you. He wanted to talk to you about Nanette. He wanted to tell you that he was sorry that he lied to you about following Nanette to North Avenue. He wanted to tell you that Nanette let him drive her home because he persuaded her that North Avenue at night was dangerous."

"But I hadn't been home for days! I was staying at Grabowski's!" Maxine said.

"Aaron didn't know that," said Hank. "He'd been working hard in the lab and hadn't talked to anyone at Mercy Hospital. He waited outside your house for an hour. Then he drove to my office to talk to me. We had a sandwich in the park. But Grabowski says he still had time to walk to Virginia's house and hit you and Virginia over the head."

"Aaron was just in the wrong place at the wrong time," said Maxine.

"Tell Grabowski," said Hank, then changed his mind. "No, don't. He'll arrest me, too. Every time he looks at me, I feel like he's going to send me to jail."

"He won't, Hank. Anyway, I know someone who saw Nanette after Aaron the night Nanette died."

"Who?" asked Hank.

"Charlie."

Hank looked surprised. "Charlie? The Ph.D. student who worked with you and Virginia at Marquette? Nanette hardly knew him. Nanette only invited Charlie to our last pool party because he was a friend of Virginia's. That's what Nanette told me."

"That wasn't true. Nanette knew Charlie very well," said Maxine. "Nanette went to his lab a few times to talk to him. She called him after Aaron took her home the night she died. Charlie was still at the lab. He went to your house to pick her up."

"So Charlie was the last person to see Nanette before she was poisoned?" Hank frowned.

"Yes," replied Maxine. "Nanette had left her car parked on North Avenue. I think she let Aaron take her home because he wouldn't go away unless she got into his car. But she wanted her car. So Nanette phoned Charlie at the lab and asked him to take her back to North Avenue."

"Why not call a taxi?" Hank asked.

Maxine thought carefully. "There must have been a

good reason. Maybe she needed to talk to Charlie about something."

Hank looked confused. "Why did she want to go back to North Avenue?"

"I don't know," Maxine said. "But I have a strong feeling that Nanette wanted to do something that night on North Avenue."

"So Charlie drove to my house, picked up my wife, and drove her to North Avenue."

"Yes," nodded Maxine.

"Then Charlie brought the poison with him from the lab," said Hank. "Charlie must have saved some poison from your experiments. He killed Nanette. Then you came to his lab and started asking questions. He got nervous. So he tried to kill you, three times. Then Virginia got suspicious about what he was doing. So he tried to kill Virginia, too."

"No! Wait! Hank! I didn't say that Charlie killed Nanette. I just said that Charlie saw her after Aaron."

Hank wasn't listening. He opened the door. "I'm going to find Charlie."

"Wait!" But the door closed. Maxine felt panic. Hank might do something dangerous when he found Charlie! Charlie was a quiet person. He only cared about his work. He didn't have many friends. He liked Nanette because she talked to him and made him feel important. Why would Charlie poison Nanette? And would Charlie try to kill Maxine? Charlie and Maxine had been friends for years!

On the other hand, Charlie didn't like Virginia. Virginia had stopped Charlie from getting his Ph.D. for years. If

Virginia were gone, Charlie could get his Ph.D., get his own research money, and get Virginia's lab. Had Charlie changed Virginia's research reports to make her look bad? Had Virginia found out? That would be a reason for Charlie to attack Virginia. But Maxine tried to imagine Charlie hiding in Virginia's garage and hitting Virginia and Maxine on the head. It didn't seem possible. And how was that connected to Nanette?

Maxine thought and thought. She thought about the other people connected to this case: Hank, Aaron, Lavelle.

Lavelle! She had told Maxine to go to 24th and North Avenue and Maxine had done that. But she hadn't yet spoken to the woman she had met there. The woman had said she had a phone number that was connected to the room above the grocery. Maxine grabbed her purse and pulled out everything. She was looking for the paper where she had written the woman's phone number. She pulled out the photos she had shown to Lavelle and the phone number. She called the number. The woman answered.

"Yes, I have the number. Wait a second. I'll get it," she said to Maxine.

While she waited, Maxine looked at the photos. In one, Nanette had her arms around Aaron. Charlie was watching. Virginia and Hank were standing behind them, talking. Was this the photo of all the people that Lavelle had been talking about?"

"Here's the number," said the woman on the phone.

Maxine wrote it down. She couldn't believe it. It was the phone number of Charlie's lab! Why did this woman have Charlie's lab phone number? How was this connected to Nanette? Then the phone rang.

"Grabowski?" Maxine shouted into the phone.

"Kareena," a quiet voice answered. "I called to find out how you are."

Suddenly Maxine knew the answer. She remembered the white spots on Lavelle's arm when she came to the ER. She suddenly knew why Nanette was killed. And she knew how. One question to Dr. Kareena Singh made her certain. "Have you seen any cases of leprosy lately?" she asked.

"Yes," Kareena replied. "Have you seen it in the ER, too?"

Maxine hung up quickly. She phoned Charlie at the Marquette lab. There was no answer, but maybe Charlie was busy and couldn't answer the phone.

The phone rang. It was Grabowski. "Hank's going to Marquette," Maxine shouted. "He thinks Charlie killed Nanette. I'm going there now," she said.

"Stay right where you are!" Grabowski shouted.

But Maxine hung up the phone. Then she got out of bed and put on her clothes, hurried out of the hospital, and got into a taxi. The taxi dropped her on the street near the Marquette biochemistry building. A white Mercedes was parked in front of the biochemistry building. Hank's car.

The building was dark. Voices were coming from Charlie's lab. She opened the door quietly. Hank was inside. His back was to the door. Charlie and Virginia were facing Hank. They were looking at something that Hank had in his hand.

"I didn't kill Nannette," Charlie said. His voice shook. "The last time I saw Nanette was Sunday, the night she died. She phoned me here at the lab about 11:30 PM. She was at her house. She said her car was parked on North Avenue. She wanted her car. She asked me to drive her there."

"Why did she call you?" Hank asked. "Why didn't she call a taxi?"

"When she phoned, she wanted to talk to Virginia, but I told her that Virginia had gone home. So she asked me to come. Then in the car, she kept asking more questions about Virginia's research."

"Stop talking about Virginia!" Hank shouted. "You came to our house and you killed her."

"No!" Charlie shouted. "I drove Nanette to the corner of 24th Street and North Avenue and left her by her car. That was the last time I ever saw her. That was just before midnight. I didn't know until yesterday that she died right after I left her!"

"You're lying," Hank said.

Hank raised his hand. He was holding a gun. Charlie looked at Virginia. "Virginia, help me!"

Virginia said nothing.

Maxine pushed the door open. "No!" she shouted. As she entered Charlie pushed Hank, hard. Hank fell down. He hit his head on the table and lay on the floor without moving. The gun also lay on the floor. Charlie reached for the gun, but Virginia picked it up. She pointed it at Charlie.

Chapter 17   *Maxine finds the truth*

"Put the gun down, Virginia," said Maxine quietly. Then she heard footsteps running up the stairs. Suddenly Grabowski came through the door. He was holding a gun.

"Give me the gun," Grabowski told Virginia.

Virginia didn't move. "Charlie killed Nanette. Arrest him," she said.

Maxine shook her head. "Before you do that, Grabowski, read Virginia's research reports. Ask her to show you the new lab refrigerator and mice, that she bought with her research money."

"They're at my house, in my basement laboratory," said Virginia.

"No they aren't, Virginia. But there are some things in your house that Grabowski will want to see. Like your secret research reports about your leprosy experiments on people."

Virginia stared at Maxine. She moved the gun to point at her. "You killed Nanette, Maxine. Then you told Hank that Charlie killed Nanette."

"Maxine," said Charlie. "Did you tell Hank that I killed Nanette?"

"No," Maxine said, watching Virginia's gun. "I told him you saw Nanette after Aaron did. But you weren't the last person to see Nanette before she swallowed the poison. Virginia was. Virginia poisoned Nanette."

"What!" Charlie gasped.

"Virginia had a big secret. Nanette found out," said Maxine. "It was a secret that would have ruined Virginia, forever."

"Is that true, Virginia?" asked Charlie.

Virginia didn't answer.

Maxine said to Virginia, "Were you shocked, Virginia, when Nanette walked into your little room on North Avenue? Did you recognize her in that red wig and leather miniskirt?"

"How did you find out?" asked Virginia.

"A woman called Lavelle – one of the women you gave the pills to – recognized you from a photo," explained Maxine. "At first, I thought Lavelle was looking at Charlie in the photo. But she was looking at you."

Virginia didn't notice that Grabowski was moving slowly behind her. Maxine and Charlie moved toward the open door to the hall. Maxine kept talking to Virginia.

"You wrote reports to the university about your new drug, Virginia," Maxine said. "You said you were testing your new drug on mice. But you lied."

Maxine moved closer to the door. She kept talking so that Virginia would not look at Grabowski.

Maxine said, "Then I phoned you to say I was coming to visit you at home, Virginia. You thought I knew about your room above the grocery on North Avenue. So you waited in your garage and you hit me on the head. When you heard the police coming, you hit yourself on the head and lay down on the floor."

Virginia shook her head. "You're crazy."

"You attacked me at the tennis club. You came into the club when the receptionist was away from her desk. And later you waited in my car and put a belt round my neck." Maxine moved closer to the door and kept talking. "You went to that room over the grocery and you paid Lavelle and other people there a lot of money – your research money. You didn't tell them you were giving them leprosy. If Marquette University Research Review Committee found out that you were giving people leprosy, your career would be finished. But Nanette found out, didn't she?"

"Yes," said Virginia. "Nanette went to North Avenue to find out about how people in a rough neighbourhood live – for her social work degree. She met Lavelle. Lavelle brought her to my room above the grocery."

"So that's where you went every week," said Charlie.

"I went one night a week. I couldn't go more than that because I didn't want anyone to know what I was doing."

"Lavelle got a lot of money from you," said Maxine. "You paid her to get leprosy. That was why she had white spots on her arm. First you gave her an injection to get leprosy. Then you tested her blood to make sure she had it. Then you paid her to take your new drug, a pill, to see if it cured the leprosy."

"That's right. There were twenty-five other women. They had to take one pill each week. Then I gave them a blood test."

"Lavelle brought Nanette one night. Right?" Maxine asked.

"Yes. Nanette walked into my room over the grocery. She was wearing that black leather skirt and that red wig. Nanette thought I didn't recognize her. But I did," said Virginia. She kept pointing the gun at Maxine.

Maxine kept talking, so that Virginia would not see that Grabowski was getting closer to her.

"Nanette didn't yet know what you were doing in the room on North Avenue. So Nanette came here, to your lab at Marquette, to find out. Didn't she?" Maxine asked.

"Yes. Nanette came here several times," Virginia replied. "She asked me about leprosy and about my research. She came when I wasn't here and she asked Charlie a lot of questions about my research. Charlie thought she liked him. He told me that she asked about my research. At the last party at her house, she kept asking me how I knew whether my new drug worked."

"When did Nanette figure out what you were doing?" Maxine asked.

"The night she died," Virginia replied. "She came to 24th Street and North Avenue, wearing that red wig. She came into my room over the grocery. She said she was Lavelle's neighbor. She told me she had got an injection from me the week before and that she now needed the pill. She probably thought she could hide the pill and find out what it was later. But I pretended I didn't know her and I made her take the pill while I watched, just like I did with the other women. But her pill had tetrodotoxin in it."

"So you killed her?" Maxine said.

"Yes," Virginia went on. "Before you left Marquette, I stole a few drops of your solution and put drops of water in their place. I was worried that Charlie knew that I was experimenting on humans. I thought I might have to give him the poison. Charlie had searched my desk and kept trying to find out what I was doing."

"Why did Nanette swallow the poisoned pill?"

"Why not? It looked like the pills I had given everyone. Nothing bad happened to them. Maybe she thought one pill wouldn't harm her. I think she planned to come back another night with Hank and show him what I was doing."

"But it was too late," said Maxine. "Nanette only had a short time to live."

Grabowski was now close to Virginia. He grabbed the gun. "You're under arrest for the murder of Nanette Myer. You have the right to remain silent . . ."

Chapter 18   *Post mortem*

Maxine, Grabowski, Shirley, Kareena, and Charlie were sitting in a restaurant near Mercy Hospital having lunch.

"When did you know that Virginia was the murderer?" asked Kareena.

"I made the connection when I was sitting in the hospital, thinking about all the people in this case," said Maxine. "The last clue was the phone number that I got when I called the woman I had met on the street by the grocery at 24th and North Avenue."

"Whose phone number was it?" asked Shirley.

"It was the number of the lab that Charlie and Virginia shared. As soon as I saw the number, I knew either Virginia or Charlie had killed Nanette. Then Kareena called. I knew then that Virginia poisoned Nanette."

"How?" asked Shirley.

"When I heard Kareena's voice, I suddenly saw the connection between Virginia, Nanette, and the room over the grocery. The connection was leprosy."

"How did you know that?" asked Shirley.

"A week before, Lavelle had come into the ER. I saw the marks of leprosy on her arms. I didn't know that Lavelle had leprosy then. But when Kareena called me in the hospital, I remembered that a month before, she had told me that one of her patients in the North Avenue clinic had leprosy. I remembered the white spots I saw on Lavelle's arms. And I remembered that Virginia was doing experiments with leprosy drugs.

"So when Kareena called me in the hospital, I asked her if she had seen any more cases of leprosy. When she said yes, I was sure that Virginia was using that room over the grocery on North Avenue. She gave people leprosy and then she gave them her drug. The drug did work. But some of the women didn't come back to take all the medicine. Virginia had to tell them a phone number to call in case they got leprosy and got sick. But the women didn't know the signs of leprosy. Kareena did."

Charlie added: "Virginia couldn't give them her own office or home phone because someone might have found out her secret. So she gave them the lab number and told them to call at certain times when she knew she'd be there to answer the phone."

"So that's the end of Virginia's career," said Kareena. "And what about yours, Maxine? Are you going back to your own research at Marquette, or will you stay at Mercy Hospital ER?"

Maxine smiled. "I think I like working at Mercy Hospital ER."

Grabowski smiled at Maxine. "And I liked working with you on this case. Now that it's over, would you like to go out with me on a real date?"

"What did you have in mind?" she asked.

"Let's go bowling," he suggested.

Maxine laughed. "Grabowski, you're such a romantic!"

Cambridge English Readers

Look out for other titles in the series:

Level 5

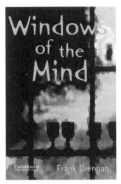

Death in the Dojo
by Sue Leather

Reporter Jate Jensen is investigating the death of a karate master in a 'dojo', a karate training room, in London. Another death quickly follows that leads Jensen to Japan, and to a crime committed thirty years earlier.

Windows of the Mind
by Frank Brennan

Five stories about the senses. We meet a broadcaster whose blindness is her power, a war hero who hates noise, a wine-taster who has an accident, a lecturer who learns Tai Chi, and a journalist who can smell a good story.

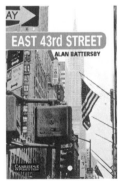

Jungle Love *by Margaret Johnson*

On holiday in the Caribbean, Lisa and Jennifer are both attracted to Ian. And Ian likes both of them. But what about his girlfriend, Caroline? And then there's Pete . . .

East 43rd Street
by Alan Battersby

It's Christmas in New York and Private Investigator Nathan Marley is hired to reclaim a briefcase of jewelry from Grand Central station. Marley soon finds himself involved in a case of fraud, computer hacking and kidnap.

Level 6

Deadly Harvest
by Carolyn Walker

Chief Inspector Jane Honeywell is a city detective in a sleepy country town who wonders why she's moved there. But then the rural peace and quiet is suddenly disturbed by a particularly horrible murder, and Jane starts the dangerous pursuit of the killer, or killers.

Frozen Pizza and other slices of life *by Antoinette Moses*

These highly enjoyable stories offer eight slices of life in England today. The themes covered include food, the media, immigration, student life, football hooliganism, inner-city problems, leisure activities and the countryside.

Trumpet Voluntary
by Jeremy Harmer

A musician disappears leaving only a strange e-mail message behind her. Her husband, in a desperate search to find her, revisits their shared past and has to face up to some unpleasant realities, before trying to rebuild his life. His journey of discovery takes us across the world to Rio and deep into the human heart.

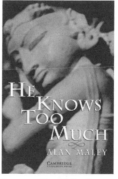

He Knows Too Much
by Alan Maley

An English executive in India, Dick Sterling, is dismissed after he tries to uncover corruption within his company. When his marriage breaks up he returns to India to seek the truth behind his dismissal. There, he is forced to choose between love and revenge.

95